WILLIAM SHAKESPEARE
and His Plays

The Globe Theater in the days of Shakespeare

Immortals of Literature

William Shakespeare
and His Plays

by Charles Haines

FRANKLIN WATTS, INC.
575 LEXINGTON AVENUE
NEW YORK, N.Y. 10022

For C. E. H.

FIRST PRINTING

Copyright © 1968 by Franklin Watts, Inc.

Library of Congress Catalog Card Number: 68-10337

PRINTED IN THE UNITED STATES OF AMERICA

Contents

WILLIAM SHAKESPEARE
and His Plays

Preface

Dante, Michelangelo, Rembrandt, Mozart, Beethoven, Tolstoy, Shakespeare: these are the names of some of the world's greatest men. They were artists, which is to say that they were creators.

What purpose does art serve? What good is it? Can Michelangelo's statue of Moses cure a disease? Can Beethoven's Third Symphony put a stop to the horrors of war? Not directly, of course, but indirectly, yes. Art, in the true sense of the word, is man's chief hope for survival and happiness.

The painful and evil aspects of man's existence involve decay, destruction, and death. Sickness and disease, floods, earthquakes, famine, fire, and, above all, war—these are the calamities that afflict man. Some of them he brings on himself; others seem to be brought on him by accident or destiny. Whatever their cause, they have it in common that they bring pain, that they destroy, and kill.

1

The true artist gives life. He does not simply construct; he does not only rearrange elements into original and pleasing combinations. He creates *ex novo,* anew and afresh.

It is the desire and the ability to create that makes the artist not only great but indispensable. More than anyone else, it is the artist that is dedicated to halting the onrush of destruction.

The principal act of creation is, of course, procreation, the birth of the child. This transmission of life from generation to generation remains one of the world's miracles and mysteries. Doctors and scientists can tell us much about anatomy and genetics and the mechanics of birth and growth; no one can tell us what life is, how we happen to have it, and how it can be passed on. No one has yet been able to explain the original cause of what we call life.

In the same way, it is not possible to explain art. It is not possible to explain, either, what love is—and it is love that leads to the transmission of life—nor why it comes about. As we cannot explain how and why man can pass on the gift of life to those that become his children, so we cannot explain how some artistic creations contain the breath of life. Why have Hamlet and Othello and Macbeth survived, to be known and loved, by fifteen generations of persons, when other characters in other plays by lesser writers than Shakespeare have vanished out of memory within ten years, or five years, of their appearance?

The capacity to create what lasts is the artist's ability. To be able to create something—a character,

2

a scene, a melody—that defies decay and death, to create what resists destruction, is to be an artist.

Shakespeare is universally thought of as one of the greatest of all artists. What he wrote has lasted now for more than three hundred and fifty years. His words are for the most part as fresh and new and touching today as they were at the moment that he wrote them. The study of art may not explain to us what art is, but we are bound to try to determine what art is *not*. We do well to learn as much as we can about an artist's life in the hope of discovering even a little more about where the gift of creation comes from. We would do well to remember that the mind, the reason, alone will never lead us to an explanation or a full understanding of art. No one ever fell in love for a reason that he or she thoroughly understood and could analyze. In the same way, no one ought to approach art—creation—with the mind only. Art is principally a matter of the pulses, of the feelings, of the heart.

Much research has been done, and yet little is known about the life of Shakespeare. We are unsure of even the major events of his life. I have tried in the following pages to put down what we do know with some certainty, those very few facts on which most modern scholars find themselves more or less in agreement. I have dealt, very briefly, with some of the plays. The opinions and the remarks that I have ventured about them are my own—as far, that is, as there can be a personal opinion about works so often considered and discussed as Shakespeare's plays. But I must mention a particular debt of gratitude to Dr. Luciana Pozzi for several ideas that in the course of private conversation she has passed on to me.

I want to record here my thanks to Mrs. D. K. Wood. She patiently typed and retyped the manuscript, and made many useful suggestions. I doubt very much that the book ever would have been completed without her help.

Carleton University,   C. H.

Ottawa, Canada.
August, 1967.

1. Shakespeare in Stratford

William Shakespeare was born on April 22 or 23, 1564, in the town of Stratford-on-Avon in the county of Warwickshire, England. We do not know the exact date of his birth. English law at the time, though, required that children be baptized as soon as possible after they were born, and Shakespeare was baptized in Holy Trinity Church, Stratford, on April 26, 1564. The entry in the Stratford parish register reads, *Gulielmus filius Johannes Shakespeare*. The vicar of Holy Trinity—a man named John Bretchgirdle—probably made the entry and baptized the baby.

Stratford-on-Avon was neither a very large nor a very important town in the England of 1564. Its population numbered about two thousand. The nearest city of any size was Worcester, twenty-five miles away. Stratford had no cathedral, and no university; it was neither a major port nor a busy manufacturing town. Yet it must have been a beautiful community, and a pleasant one to live in, when Shakespeare was a boy.

Just to the east of it flowed the lazy River Avon, over which a handsome, arched bridge had been built about the year 1500. At the foot of the causeway that led to the bridge, just at the entrance to the town, were two inns: the Bear and the Swan. The courtyards of these inns were used now and then for dances, and sometimes for performances of plays and exhibitions of acrobatics put on by troupes of strolling players.

Many of the houses in Stratford were, of course, built in what we now call the Elizabethan style. They were made partly of wood, and partly of brick or plaster. The houses fronted directly on the streets, but very often there was a garden or an orchard behind them. The center of town was the corner where Bridge Street crossed High Street. Here, there was a sort of clock tower called High Cross. Near it, tradesmen displayed their wares on market days; and here, too, there was a whipping post at which beggars, vagabonds, and delinquents were punished from time to time. Some of the streets in Stratford had simple, direct names which are rarely used any more in the twentieth century: Bull Lane, Sheep Street, Swine Street. The house in which Shakespeare was born stood on a street more simply named Henley Street because it led out of town to the neighboring village of Henley. The house has been remodeled and rebuilt several times since 1564, but every year tens of thousands of people make a trip to see it: the birthplace of one of the greatest writers that ever lived.

Johannes (John) Shakespeare, the poet's father, had been a country boy. His father in turn—Richard

Shakespeare—had been a farmer near Snitterfield, a village five miles north of Stratford. John Shakespeare evidently decided, as a young man, not to become a farmer, and he moved into Stratford, where he set himself up as a glover. Not very much is known about the life of John Shakespeare, but clearly he was an ambitious and a hardworking man. A few years after moving to Stratford, he expanded his business, and became a dealer in wool and timber. He was elected an alderman of the town in 1565, the bailiff (or mayor) in 1568, and, in 1571, chief alderman. It seems, too, that although John Shakespeare was for a time a prosperous businessman and a successful politician, he had never learned to read or write; at least, there is no record of so much as a signature by him.

About 1577, for unknown reasons, John Shakespeare's career seems to have taken a turn for the worse. He quit politics and sold some of the property that he owned, probably to raise money. What had happened? Had he lost his savings in a financial investment? Had he fallen sick? We do not know. We know only that several years after John Shakespeare's career had begun to slip downhill, his son left Stratford, perhaps for London, just as his father had left Snitterfield for Stratford. Perhaps, then, Shakespeare began his career as an actor and a writer partly out of a desire to help his father financially. We do know one other major fact in John Shakespeare's life. In 1568, he applied to the College of Heralds for a grant of arms. (A coat of arms was a status symbol in the sixteenth century.) The arms were awarded to him, but

7

only after thirty years had passed; and John Shakespeare did not live to enjoy his new dignity for very long. On September 8, 1601, he was buried in the Stratford churchyard. His son was then thirty-seven years old, and one of the best-known writers in England.

Shakespeare's mother was Mary Arden, one of eight children of Robert Arden, a wealthy landowner near Snitterfield. Even less is known about Shakespeare's mother than about his father. We do know that she and John Shakespeare were married in 1558, and that the couple had eight children. William was the third child, and the first son. Mary Arden Shakespeare was buried in Stratford on September 9, 1608.

Of the Shakespeares' eight children, only William became famous. In fact, only five survived childhood. Gilbert was born in 1566, and died in 1612. Joan was born in 1569. She married a Stratford man named William Hart, a hatter, and they had four children. The descendants of Thomas, the third child, are the only persons living today known to be directly related to William Shakespeare. Joan was buried in Stratford in 1646. Richard Shakespeare was born in 1574, and died in 1613. Edmund was born in 1580, and perhaps he, too, went to London and became an actor. There is no mention anywhere of his career, but a note written on New Year's Eve, 1607, by the sexton of St. Saviour's Church in London, tells of the burial on that day of "Edmund Shakespeare, a Player. . ."

Until 1580, when he was sixteen years old, William Shakespeare was probably a normal English village schoolboy. If he showed any signs of genius as a child,

8

none have been recorded. We assume that he went to the local free grammar school, starting lessons there, as the other Stratford boys did, at the age of seven. He learned to read and write and then went on to the thorough study of Latin language and literature, the standard school courses of the day. At that time the Stratford school employed only two teachers—a young master for the smaller boys, and an older, more experienced man to teach the upper classes.

Shakespeare graduated from the Stratford school at the age of sixteen, but he did not go on to a university. His name does not appear anywhere in the records of either Oxford or Cambridge, the only two universities in England at the time. Since he did not continue his formal education, he probably went to work. But what kind of work did he do? And since he spent his mature life as an actor and a writer, he must have done a great deal of reading, and he must have gone to see plays. What books did he read? Where did he see plays performed?

We do not know what job Shakespeare took after he left school, because there are no documents, records, or letters to tell us. Some people say that he became a butcher. John Aubrey, a seventeenth-century biographer, wrote this about him:

His father was a butcher, and I have been told heretofore by some of the neighbours, that when he was a boy, he exercised his father's trade, but when he killed a calf, he would do it in a high style and make a speech.

9

This is a colorful picture, and some people like to believe that it is also a true one. But Aubrey was not always a strictly accurate biographer. He tended to record unproved statements based on rumors and gossip. For one thing, John Shakespeare was not principally a butcher. In all likelihood, the story of Shakespeare, the poetic young meatcutter, is not a true one.

Other people say that Shakespeare went to work in the office of one of Stratford's lawyers. This seems more believable. Shakespeare's father, with his numerous political connections, could easily have helped his son to find a job as a lawyer's clerk. If Shakespeare did spend any time in a law office, we could more easily account for the frequent references in his plays to the law, lawyers, judges, and legal language. Perhaps he even worked for Stratford's leading lawyer, a man named, appropriately enough, William Court.

If Shakespeare did work in William Court's office, probably Court from time to time lent him books to read. It is obvious that Shakespeare read, and read widely, and that he remembered clearly a great many of the things that he had read. There was no lending library in Stratford in 1580. If Shakespeare's father really was unable to read and write, it is unlikely that there would have been many books about the Shakespeare household. But one of the lawyers of the town, or the vicar of the church, or perhaps one of the schoolmasters, would have been able to lend books to Shakespeare.

What books would he have read? Undoubtedly he read Chaucer's *Canterbury Tales*, for Chaucer was both a respected and a popular writer in Elizabethan

England. The *Canterbury Tales* would have been easily obtainable even in a small country town. He surely also read the poetry of Wyatt and Surrey, which had been published in 1557. Wyatt and Surrey were the modern poets of the day, up-to-date, nonconformist, romantic young men. They wrote English poetry in the Italian style, and their lines were both musical and passionate. Above all, Shakespeare must have read Sir Thomas North's translation of *The Lives of the Noble Grecians and Romans*, by Plutarch. Although this great book has fallen somewhat into neglect today, in the late sixteenth century it was one of the cornerstones of any educated man's library. It came out in 1579, and by 1603 it had gone into nine editions. It told, in North's vivid English, the story of the lives of twenty-three famous ancient Greeks, and of twenty-three famous ancient Romans. We know for certain that at some time Shakespeare read North's Plutarch, because he drew on it for the plots of four of his plays, and on several occasions (particularly in *Antony and Cleopatra*), he incorporated whole sentences from it into his own text.

Surely Shakespeare also read the Bible, and probably such works as *The Chronicles of England, Scotland, and Ireland,* by Raphael Holinshed; *Chroniques,* by the French writer Jean Froissart; and the *Essais,* by Michel de Montaigne. But it was not reading alone that made the Stratford glover's son into one of the world's greatest playwrights. Shakespeare also surely came in touch with plays and with the theater.

London was the center of such theatrical activity as

11

there was in England when Shakespeare was a boy, but companies of strolling actors, at various times and for various reasons, toured the smaller towns to give plays, and to put on exhibitions of acrobatics, singing, and dancing. Many towns in England celebrated two or three of the major holidays of the year with pageants which would include parades and dancing and often a dramatic sketch based on the life of St. George, or perhaps of Robin Hood. Shakespeare almost certainly saw some of these pageants as a boy in Stratford. In 1569, John Shakespeare himself issued a permit to a troupe of strolling players to put on a play in the town. In 1572, and again in 1575, Queen Elizabeth made a visit to Kenilworth, to the castle of the Earl of Leicester. Entertainment of all kinds was provided for her: parades, fireworks, a water pageant, and, of course, plays. All of these spectacles were open to the public, and Kenilworth was only twelve miles from Stratford. John Shakespeare may well have taken his son there to see the festivities, and perhaps to get a glimpse of the great queen herself.

We know that troupes of actors went to Stratford during the winters of 1576–77, 1581–82, and in March of 1584. The 1584 appearance was a momentous one. A young man of eighteen had just joined the troupe that visited Stratford. His name was Edward Alleyn, and he was to become one of the most famous actors of the next fifty years. Shakespeare could not have helped but be impressed by Alleyn. Not long after Alleyn's performance, Shakespeare left Stratford and set out to make his fortune in the world.

But work and reading and fascination with the theater were not the only factors in Shakespeare's life after 1580. He was also in love. Some time before November, 1582, he had fallen in love with a girl who lived near Stratford. Her name was Anne Hathaway. Shakespeare was eighteen in 1582, and Anne Hathaway was twenty-six. Perhaps the difference in the couple's ages is a kind of proof of the maturity, intelligence, and ardor of the future playwright. But the difference in ages was not the only unusual thing in the story of Shakespeare's courtship and marriage.

On November 28, 1582, a marriage license was applied for, to permit the wedding of Anne Hathaway and William Shakespeare. On the day before, however, a marriage license had been issued for the wedding of William Shakespeare and a certain Anne Whateley.

It is rather difficult to explain this strange happening. Anne Whateley is a very shadowy figure. Her name appears only this once in any public record book. We know nothing at all about her, except that she seems to have been the girl whom, according to this official document, Shakespeare intended to marry. It is, of course, possible that the registry clerk made a mistake on November 27, and wrote "Whateley" for "Hathaway," then silently corrected his error the next day by reissuing the license correctly marked. But some people continue to think that Anne Whateley did exist; that Shakespeare was a tempestuous and attractive young man; that he may have been "engaged" to two girls at the same time; that the story of his marriage, if it were fully known, would be a complex tale of requited and unrequited love.

Shakespeare did marry—he refers to his wife in his will—but there is no record of when or where the marriage actually took place. He almost certainly did marry Anne Hathaway, for the first biography of Shakespeare, written in 1709, mentions that his wife was the daughter of one "Hathaway." In the Stratford parish register for May 26, 1583, there is also a record of the baptism in Holy Trinity Church of "Susanna, daughter to William Shakespeare."

Shakespeare was a husband and father before he saw the performance by the great Edward Alleyn; before, probably, he had made up his mind to try to make his living in the theater; and before he set out to make his fortune away from the town of Stratford.

2. Shakespeare in London

In 1585, Shakespeare became a father for the second and third time. On February 2, Hamnet and Judith, his twin son and daughter, were baptized in Stratford. After this date nothing is recorded about Shakespeare for seven years. Then, in September, 1592, a London playwright named Robert Greene referred to him, somewhat jealously, as a popular and important writer and man of the theater.

What did Shakespeare do between February, 1585, and September, 1592? Many people have tried to make intelligent guesses about these seven silent years. Some have said that he traveled, spending time in Italy, France, or Germany. How else, they wonder, could he have found out all that he tells us in his plays about the life, literature, and traditions of the Continent? Others say that he went straight to London with the intention of making his fortune there. Still others argue that he left Stratford for London, not to make his fortune, but in great haste because he had been caught stealing rabbits and deer from a neighboring nobleman's property.

It has often been said, too, that when Shakespeare got to London, he took the first job that was offered to him: one as a horse-holder outside a theater. From this lowly beginning, he is supposed to have worked his way rapidly upward in the theatrical world, becoming first an actor, then a writer, and finally a producer, returning to Stratford, rich and famous, twenty-five years after he had left it. Still other people believe that Shakespeare went away from Stratford in 1586 or 1587 to become a country schoolmaster, or perhaps to take a position as tutor in some nobleman's household; and that after two or three years, he moved to London and immediately found work as a writer and editor of plays. But whether Shakespeare really ever was a deer-stealer or a horse-holder or a schoolmaster, we do not know. There is no reliable evidence to prove the truth of any of these various stories.

Let us try, however, to reconstruct Shakespeare's life between 1585 and 1592, gathering all the facts that might seem to have some bearing on this period.

We know that the actor Edward Alleyn played in Stratford in 1584. We know that Shakespeare himself became an actor. We know that Shakespeare wrote plays, and that nearly half of the plays that he wrote were set in Italy or in ancient Rome. It is certain, also, that he wrote two long poems, both of which he dedicated to the young Earl of Southampton. And Shakespeare, later in his life, was highly respected by many people, both as a writer and as a person. These statements are all facts; there is historical proof for each one of them.

From the facts that we do know, this is what *might* have happened to Shakespeare during those seven silent years. In March, 1584, he saw a performance given in Stratford by a company of actors known as Worcester's Men. One of the actors was Edward Alleyn, and Shakespeare very much enjoyed the performance. Not particularly rich, but both imaginative and ambitious, he decided that more than anything else he would like to find work with a theater company. He approached some of the actors, perhaps Alleyn himself, at the end of the performance. He told them who he was, and what he wanted to do. They suggested that the best way for a young man with no experience to get into the theater was by first obtaining the patronage of some nobleman, for all actors in Elizabethan England were ostensibly under the protection of various noblemen. Shakespeare was told to seek a patron.

The people that gave this advice probably did not take the young man's ambitions very seriously. Shakespeare, however, did what had been suggested. He started to look for a patron. He wrote letters to various noblemen who had a reputation for generosity. His father, as a former mayor, may have been able to persuade the Earl of Leicester at Kenilworth to help in the search. After a number of months (during which Shakespeare continued to work in William Court's law office), a reply came back from the young Earl of

17

Southampton, who was, at the time, a student at Cambridge University. Since his father had died in 1581, he had already succeeded to the title. A brilliant and attractive youth, he was fabulously rich as well. Southampton said that he did not know much about theater, but that he could offer Shakespeare a job as a schoolmaster in a village in Hampshire, near his own house at Titchfield. He also said that if all went well, he would invite Shakespeare to join his retinue, some time after 1589, when he had himself graduated from Cambridge.

Shakespeare accepted the job in Hampshire. Even though it meant leaving Stratford, his father, and his wife and children, it would have been foolish for him to have refused the nobleman's offer, especially since his father had fallen on hard times. During the three or four years that Shakespeare spent as a teacher, he had access to Southampton's house and to his library; and thus, he was able to spend a great deal of his free time in reading.

After Southampton had graduated from Cambridge, true to his word, he found a place for Shakespeare in his household. He also employed at about the same time, as his tutor in Italian, a certain John Florio, one of the greatest scholars of the day. With Florio, Shakespeare was able to read the works of the great Italian writers: Dante, Boccaccio, Bandello, Ariosto, and Cinzio. Florio also told him something of the history of the Italian Renaissance, as well as particulars of the Italian drama of the day, or *commedia dell'arte*, as it was called. Thus Shakespeare came into close contact with one of the most powerful noblemen of England, and with one of the greatest scholars of the age.

About 1590, urged on by both Southampton and Florio, Shakespeare tried his own hand at writing. The result was a play based on the history of England at the time of King Henry VI. He sent the play to London, to the manager of a company of actors known as the Earl of Strange's Men. The manager, of course, was careful to deal respectfully with a manuscript submitted by a protégé of the Earl of Southampton. In any case, the play was not at all a bad one. In fact, it was much better than many of the plays that were being performed in London at that time. (This first play may have been the work that we now know as *Henry VI, Part Two*.) Strange's Men accepted it for production. Shakespeare, thus encouraged, reminded the earl that his ambition had always been to work with a theatrical company. He asked for permission to leave the earl's retinue and to join Strange's Men. Southampton gave permission. He also advanced Shakespeare some money with which to buy a share, or part ownership, in the company. By 1591, Shakespeare was in London, connected with the Earl of Strange's Men, ready to work with a theater company as an actor, a writer, or an editor. His ambition had been fulfilled.

Of course, this story is almost pure guesswork based on a few known facts. Yet, if some of Shakespeare's time between 1585 and 1592 had been spent in this way, in association with both Southampton and Florio, we could explain many things which otherwise are not easily explained: his interest in and knowledge of Italy; the wide reading that he must have done; his knowledge of court etiquette. We could account for the tradition that Southampton at some time gave Shakespeare £1,000 "to go through with a purchase," and we could account for Shakespeare's later having dedicated both of his nondramatic poems to the young earl. These two poems were *Venus and Adonis,* written in 1592, and *The Rape of Lucrece,* 1593. The dedication of *The Rape of Lucrece* sounds more cordial and more sincere than does the language used by many poets of the time in their dedications:

TO THE RIGHT HONOURABLE, HENRY WRIOTHESLEY,

EARL OF SOUTHAMPTON, AND BARON OF TITCHFIELD.

The love I dedicate to your Lordship is without end: whereof this pamphlet, without beginning, is but a superfluous moiety. The warrant I have of your honourable disposition, not the worth of my untutor'd lines, makes it assured of acceptance. What I have done is yours; what I have to do is yours; being part in all I have, devoted yours. Were my worth greater, my duty would show greater; meantime, as it is, it is bound to your Lordship, to whom I wish long life, still length'ned with all happiness.

Your Lordship's in all duty,
WILLIAM SHAKESPEARE.

It would be fairly safe to assume on the strength of these lines alone that Southampton had been, and probably was to continue to be, both Shakespeare's patron and his good friend.

One other fact is interesting. In 1578, John Florio published a book entitled *First Fruits*. In it there is this sentence:

> We need not speak so much of love: all books are full of love, with so many authors, that it were labour lost to speak of love.

The title of one of Shakespeare's first plays is *Love's Labour's Lost*. There can be little doubt that Shakespeare made up his title by drawing on Florio's sentence. This does not, of course, prove that he knew Florio personally. It does prove, however, that he knew something of Florio's writings before 1594 when, most probably, *Love's Labour's Lost* was written.

Shakespeare certainly was in London during the summer of 1592. In September of that year, a book called *Greene's Groat's-Worth of Wit Bought With a Million of Repentance* was published. This strange and angry work had been written a few months before by Robert Greene, a bitter and impoverished dramatist. He was on his deathbed when he wrote it. He had many hard things to say about actors and other men of the theater but he singled out one person for a particularly slashing attack:

> . . . Yes, trust them not: for there is an upstart Crow, beautified with our feathers, that with his

Tyger's heart wrapped in a Player's hide, supposes he is as well able to bombast out a blank verse as the best of you: and being an absolute Johannes fac totum, is, in his own conceit, the only Shake-scene in a country.

There can be no doubt that Greene was referring to Shakespeare with these lines. The word "Shake-scene" alone would be proof of that, but the phrase "Tyger's heart wrapped in a Player's hide" is clearly a parody of a line that appears in *Henry VI, Part Three* (near the end of the first act), by Shakespeare:

O Tyger's heart wrapped in a woman's hide!

The fact that Greene attacked him so vigorously in 1592 shows that Shakespeare was well known as an actor and a writer by that time. In order for him to have become that well known, he must have been in London for at least a year by September, 1592, and also he must have already written a "hit" by then.

It is not surprising, therefore, to find in the financial records of Lord Strange's Men (some of which luckily have survived) that Shakespeare had indeed written a hit; and, what is more, that a recent performance of a play written by Greene himself, in collaboration with a certain Thomas Lodge, had been a failure. On March 3, 1592, Lord Strange's Men presented a new play, *Harey the VI*, which earned them three pounds, sixteen shillings, and eight pence, the highest receipts for any series of performances put on during their 1591–92 season. *Harey the VI* was doubtless one of

Shakespeare's three *Henry VI* plays—spelled in the company's record books with the usual carelessness that attended much Elizabethan spelling.

Shakespeare had not only broken into the charmed circle of Elizabethan dramatists and actors; he had been an immediate popular success.

3. "The Theatre"

Theater in Elizabethan England was not at all like theater in twentieth-century London or New York. Now people usually attend plays at night, buying tickets in advance, and often paying a very high price for them. They enter an auditorium, and sit in rows of more or less comfortable seats, reading their programs until the performance begins. After a time, the auditorium is darkened, the curtain goes up, and the audience sees an intricately constructed and carefully lighted set on which actors move as naturally and normally as possible, usually speaking lines in conversational, true-to-life tones of voice. While the play is going on, the audience generally is quite. A few people may make some noise unwrapping candy bars, but no one interrupts the actors, or comments out loud on the play while it is still in progress. At the end of each act, people clap as loudly or as softly as they think the play and the acting deserve; and after the last curtain call, they file slowly out of the theater.

Theater was entirely different in the London of Queen Elizabeth's day. The performances were given in the afternoon. Spectators bought their tickets a few minutes before the play was to start, and they spent one penny, or perhaps twopence or threepence for them. The theater building itself had no roof, and for most of the audience, there were no seats to sit on. The stage was not separated from the audience by a curtain or an orchestra pit, but instead it jutted out among the viewers. If a man was willing to pay a little extra, he was entitled to bring a stool and sit right up on the stage, and watch the play from there. Although the actors wore ornate and expensive costumes, there was no constructed scenery or set, and there were no intricate lighting effects. The actors did not often try to move or talk "naturally," but tended to strut and posture, and shout, rather than speak, their lines.

An Elizabethan audience often interrupted the performances with shouted comments, sometimes to praise an actor, and sometimes to abuse him. The more excitable spectators would warn an intended victim of the villain's approach, or would cheer on a favorite character engaged in a stage fight. The audience did not eat candy bars during the performance, but many people ate nuts—in fact, there are records of complaints about all the noise that people made during performances by cracking nuts with their teeth. Whether the play was a tragedy or a comedy, it was usually followed by an exhibition of tumbling or of acrobatics or by a series of songs.

Whereas today an evening at the theater is usually

considered a dignified and refined activity, theater-going in Elizabethan London was felt by many people to be rather wicked and sinful. There was constant agitation by religious and civil authorities to have all plays throughout England banned permanently. (The theaters actually were all closed in 1642, and officially kept closed until about 1660.)

Finally, there were no actresses in Elizabethan plays. All women's parts were taken by boys. This custom may have had some drawbacks, but in other ways, it may have added to the general entertainment. In many plays of the time, plots demanded that a woman dress up as a man, perhaps in order to work out some complicated scheme, or to put her lover to a "true love" test. The humor of this kind of situation often escapes modern audiences, but the Elizabethans, who were watching boys dressed up as girls dressed up as boys, undoubtedly found a great deal in it to laugh about.

Theatergoing was the modern, up-to-date, but slightly questionable, form of entertainment in Eliza-bethan London. For several centuries, plays had been performed in England, but until about 1565, they had been, for the most part, either stylized dramatic pag-eants that usually illustrated Bible stories, or slow-moving sketches meant to teach virtue and morality. These miracle plays and morality plays, as they are often called, were usually amateur performances. They were not given in a specially built theater, but in the open air, frequently in the courtyards of inns, wher-ever the actors could set up a stage. The actors themselves were not professionals but were men who earned their living as farmers, tradesmen, or craftsmen. Performances were not given regularly, but usually only on particular religious or civil holidays.

The first regular public theater building in England was put up near London in the year 1576. It was a large round structure, built mostly of wood, and it was called just "The Theatre." It stood north and west of Ludgate Hill and St. Paul's Cathedral, in a part of London known as "the liberty of Holywell." (A liberty was a small area within a county that was exempt from the power of the sheriff. Neither the mayor nor the London Corporation had any direct control over the London liberties or over what happened in them.) Its owners and builders were James Burbage (father of the actor Richard Burbage, who was to take the leading roles in many of Shakespeare's plays) and his brother-in-law, John Brayne. We do not know the name of the first play performed in the Theatre—the gala première, as it were, of all professional drama in England—but whatever play it was, it was probably performed by a group of actors known as Leicester's Men.

The Theatre was a financial success, and a second playhouse—the Curtain—was soon built near the first. It, too, prospered. Immediately, other London speculators recognized that drama was, among other things, a sound financial investment, and more theaters were opened: Blackfriars, the Rose, the Swan, and, in 1599, the theater in which many of Shakespeare's plays were staged, the Globe. All of these, however, were built in liberties.

27

There was good reason for theater owners to stay within the liberties. Since plays and theater were looked on by so many as frivolous, decadent, and an immoral waste of time, the city government would gladly have closed the Theatre, the Curtain, Blackfriars, and the others, if their authority had extended over them. Although it may seem strange that there could have been such fierce opposition to plays, it is perhaps possible to understand, if not justify, the point of view of the enemies of the theater. London, in the late sixteenth century, like many cities in many countries, lived in constant fear of epidemics of the plague. This fear was not unjustified. In 1563, 20,000 Londoners had been killed by the plague. In 1593, 11,000 died. In 1603, an epidemic killed 30,000. Since the population of metropolitan London in 1600 was about 200,000, it is easy to see what an enormous disaster the plague must have been. It was reasoned by the London civic authorities (and they were not altogether wrong) that the plague was more easily spread when large groups of people were crowded together into a small space. The theaters, therefore, were felt to represent a menace to the public health. So strong was this feeling, and so great was the pressure put on the theaters, that actors and owners agreed not to give any performances, even in the liberties of London, during those months in which a certain number of verified cases of plague deaths had been discovered.

Not only health, but also worry over political unrest made the authorities frown on theatergoing. After all, they reasoned, here were three or four thousand people gathered in one place. An agitator might well

leap onto the stage and harangue the crowd from
there, urging them to overthrow the government, to
burn the parliament buildings, to assassinate a general, or the like. Perhaps the authorities were right
to be concerned but perhaps, too, they exaggerated the
potential dangers. In any case, very few riots broke
out in the theaters. (It must be admitted, however,
that on one afternoon in 1602, admission prices were
raised at the Swan, and a spectacular operatic display
was promised. The man that had rented the theater
and advertised the entertainment simply collected the
money from the public at the doors, and then made off
with the entire take without putting on any show at
all. Understandably, the defrauded crowd did riot,
and caused considerable damage to the theater by way
of expressing its displeasure.) Only one political up-
rising of any great consequence can be directly connected to the presentation of a play: that was the Earl
of Essex' rebellion, on February 8, 1601. This strange
incident will be discussed later.

The Puritans were very much opposed to the theater.
The number of Puritans in England, and therefore the
Puritan influence, including that in the London city
government, increased sharply during Shakespeare's
lifetime. What the Puritans thought of the theater was
said vigorously and concisely by William Prynne, who
wrote his *Histrio-Mastix, The Players' Scourge*, in
1633, several years after Shakespeare had died; but
what he said was the point of view held by most of the
Puritans in England during the years between 1580
and 1660:

. . . Stage plays (the very pomps of the Devil which we renounce in baptism, if we believe the Fathers) are sinful, heathenish, lewd, ungodly spectacles, and most pernicious corruptions; condemned in all ages, as intolerable mischiefs to churches, to republics, to the manners, minds, and souls of men. And that the profession of play-poets, of stage players; together with the penning, acting and frequenting of stage-plays are unlawful, infamous and misbeseeming to Christians.

Prynne and his fellow Puritans sincerely opposed playgoing on religious and moral grounds, feeling that plays too often dealt with frivolous or immoral subjects in language that made frequent use of vulgarity and blasphemy. Some of the plays of the early years of the seventeenth century, although none by Shakespeare, perhaps deserved, at least in part, the Puritans' condemnation. The Puritans also objected to the fact that workmen and apprentices would often sneak away from their jobs, and spend the afternoon at the theater; and to the fact that the crowded theaters presented both a temptation and a potential work area for thieves, pickpockets, and even murderers.

Thus, for reasons concerned with hygiene, with politics, and with religion, the actors, dramatists, and theater owners found themselves under frequent attack. Indeed, it is probably true that drama managed to survive in England, and the theaters were able to stay open, chiefly because Queen Elizabeth, and later King James I, enjoyed plays, asked for special private performances in the palace, and paid the actors' companies well. Nominally, public performances of plays were merely rehearsals for private command performances to be given at Court. There was a special government department called the Revels Office, whose job it was to organize the court's entertainment—the Court Revels, as it was called. Thus, however harshly the theaters were attacked on the one hand, they were protected on the other by royal favor. Today's audiences can be very grateful that both Queen Elizabeth and King James I enjoyed plays so much. If they had not, probably not one of Shakespeare's dramas would ever have been written.

It has been estimated that attendance at the several theaters operating in London about the year 1600 totaled about twenty thousand persons each week, or approximately one tenth of the population of the city. Considering the number of people at the time who either could not, or absolutely would not, ever attend a play—the very young, the very old, and the Puritans formed the three largest groups—we can see that, judging by statistics alone, theatergoing was the most popular form of entertainment of the day.

None of the Elizabethan theaters to which those twenty thousand people went each week have survived, but we do have a sketch of the inside of one of them. The sketch was made of the Swan theater in 1596 by a Dutch tourist in London, Johannes De Witt. Although De Witt's original drawing has been lost, a copy had been made of it by one of his friends, a man named Arend Van Buchel, and that sketch has

31

survived. It shows that the Swan was a round, three-story building, for the most part open to the sky, resembling to a certain extent a small, present-day American baseball stadium. The inside wall of the building held three tiers of galleries, and it was here that most of the twopenny or threepenny customers sat on cushioned stools. The penny customers stood about on the unpaved ground level inside the arena, and they remained standing for the two, three, or four hours of the performance. The stage was a rectangular platform raised up to about the level of the shoulders of the groundlings (as the standees were called), and supported on two squat columns. At the back of the stage, there were two doors through which the actors made their entrances and exits. Above the doors was a sort of gallery that served for balcony or tower scenes. Undoubtedly, the actors' dressing rooms (or "tiring houses") were beyond the two doors, as was the business office of the theater. This part of the building was covered with a thatched roof, and a flag was flown from the roof on performance days and while a play was actually in progress.

The De Witt drawing shows a simple wooden bench toward the front of the stage, but no other scenery. There are three rather crudely drawn actors on stage. One is a woman (that is, a boy dressed up as a woman) sitting on a bench. A man is standing behind the bench. The third actor is a man carrying a spear, or staff, and he is evidently talking rather energetically to the other two.

Some scholars today are not altogether convinced

that De Witt (or perhaps Van Buchel) was a careful or reliable artist. They are sure, for one thing, that all Elizabethan theaters had an "inner stage" set between the two exit and entrance doors, but there is no trace of it in the De Witt sketch. They also wonder whether De Witt was right when he wrote, at the time that he made his drawing, that the Swan could "accommodate three thousand people in its seats." If he was correct, and if his figure excludes the number of groundlings, as logically it must if he speaks of "seats," then the Swan would have had a capacity of over five thousand people. It is true that the Swan was the largest of the London theaters; but even so, a theater that could put on a performance for five thousand people at one time seems to be a very large theater to have been built in a city with a total population of only two hundred thousand.

While the first public theaters were going up near London, and while Shakespeare was perhaps teaching his first lessons in a country school in Hampshire, events were taking place on the political scene that were to end in one of the most important and influential events in English history.

During the reign of Queen Elizabeth, the Protestant Reformation had been gathering force, both on the Continent and in England itself. Although Elizabeth was a very popular ruler, a certain number of people in England and elsewhere would have preferred a monarch in London who would have worked harder to maintain the power of the Roman Catholic Church.

33

These people wanted Mary, Queen of Scots, to take Elizabeth's place. They even argued that since Mary was the great-granddaughter of Henry VII of England, she had more right to the crown than had Elizabeth, who was the daughter of Henry VIII by his second wife. Spurred on by the strongly pro-Catholic King Philip II of Spain, the anti-Elizabeth group gained in strength, and threatened to unseat Elizabeth from the throne. At last, reluctantly, Elizabeth came to feel that her hand had been forced. In defense of her throne and her nation, she had Mary executed on February 8, 1587.

When King Philip heard of Mary's death, he vowed revenge. After all, he had been the husband of "Bloody" Queen Mary of England (who had died in 1558), and if pressed, he might even have argued that he, and not Elizabeth, should be ruler of England. For this reason, and also because he was angry with constant English interference in his attempts to colonize America, Philip decided to invade England. His plan was to assemble a great fleet, sail up the River Thames, and land tens of thousands of soldiers on English soil. Spain was the richest and most powerful nation in Europe. The conquest of England would be a relatively easy task.

Queen Elizabeth had two major principles by which she ruled. The first was at all times to spend as little money as possible; the second, to avoid war at almost any cost. Yet devotion to these principles did not blind her to the danger with which her country was now threatened. Subtly and silently, she went to work against Philip. First, she allowed Sir Francis Drake to make an unofficial surprise attack on Cadiz, in southern Spain, where he destroyed many of the Spanish ships that were being prepared for the invasion. Drake described the raid as "singeing the king of Spain's beard." Philip was forced to postpone his attack for a year as a result of it. Second, Elizabeth appealed to London, and to many of the English coastal towns, to contribute money, men, and ships to their country's defense. The response to her appeal was, in the case of London alone, double what she had expected. Lord Howard of Effingham, the Lord High Admiral of England, officially gathered together thirty-four manned and seaworthy vessels; and nearly fifty thousand men under arms stood ready near London to repel any attack.

July, 1588, was a month of storms at sea. Nevertheless, at three o'clock on the afternoon of July 19, the "Invincible" Spanish Armada was sighted off the coast of England. One hundred and fifty ships had sailed north from Spain, each larger by far than any of the ships that England could boast. The line of vessels stretched out for seven miles, threatening by sheer might to overthrow the whole of England with very little trouble. Proudly they anchored for the night, just outside the harbor of the city of Plymouth. The moon rose at two o'clock on the morning of July 20, and by its light the Spanish commanders saw that several small English ships had slipped out of Plymouth and were prepared to attack. The armada immediately set sail; the English pursued, nipping and firing as

35

they went. By July 28, the Spanish fleet was off Calais, and was still being harassed by the smaller and more maneuverable English ships. The plans to invade England had to be abandoned.

The English succeeded in setting fire to several of the Spanish men-of-war. Then a series of storms blew up. The armada half fled, half was driven north to Scotland. Only sixty Englishmen were killed in the various encounters with the armada; but of the one hundred and fifty Spanish ships that had sailed, only fifty ever got back to their home ports. Of the thirty thousand Spaniards that had set out, less than a third lived to tell the tale.

The defeat of the Spanish Armada changed the face and mind of the English nation. Elizabeth was secure on her throne. England had suddenly proved herself the most powerful nation in the world. A great sense of pride swept the country. The future was bright; the present was grand; the past was glorious. England was united in a feeling of delight over her own sense of strength. It was small wonder that the citizens of London were ready to eat, drink, and be merry. It was small wonder that writers came forward to praise the glories of England, and of her powerful queen.

Shakespeare, too, must have been infected by this sudden new national consciousness. The first four plays that he wrote were dramatizations of events in English history. All of them were resounding popular successes.

4. The History Plays

Shakespeare probably became part of the London theatrical world two or three years after the defeat of the Spanish Armada: perhaps late in 1590 or early in 1591. He joined the company of actors known as Strange's Men, a group made up of some of the actors that had given the first professional public performance at the Theatre in 1576. At that time they had been called Leicester's Men.

Elizabethan acting companies always used the name or title of the nobleman who was their patron. If the patron changed, so did the company's name. In 1591, Strange's Men were acting under the name and patronage of Lord Strange. He became the Earl of Derby in September, 1593, and immediately Strange's Men became Derby's Men. The Earl of Derby died soon afterward, however, and the actors found a patron in Lord Hunsdon, who was also the Lord Chamberlain, and the company became known as the Chamberlain's

Men. When the first Lord Hunsdon died in 1596, his son continued as the actors' patron, and, in 1597, he, in turn, was named Lord Chamberlain. The company that Shakespeare worked with continued to be known as the Chamberlain's Men until May, 1603, when they came under the patronage of the new king, James I. Naturally, they then were called the King's Men. Shakespeare stayed with one company for the more than twenty-five years that he was at work in London. Although the company changed its name several times, and moved from theater to theater, Shakespeare did not shift his loyalty. Even if he ever had thought of leaving the Chamberlain's Men for another group, his associates would certainly have exerted all their powers of persuasion to keep him. He was, after all, as an actor, and especially as a writer, one of their chief assets.

There were usually about twelve actors in each of the actors' companies. Four or five might be sharers, or part owners of the company. Each of the sharers was entitled to take his percentage of the profits. Besides the actors, there were hired men who worked as musicians, costume men, stagehands, and prompters, and, as well, as spear carriers in battle scenes, or as courtiers in crowd scenes. They were paid about six shillings (or twenty-seven dollars) per week. There were also the apprentices: boys who were already doing women's parts, and were learning the men's parts that they hoped to play when they were older. If a company was lucky, it also was in close touch with a writer who could write plays that would please both the

38

groundlings and the threepenny customers in the galleries. One company, called the Admiral's Men, had secured the services of the brilliant, young, erratic Christopher Marlowe. Marlowe's *Tamburlaine, Dr. Faustus,* and *Edward II* (all written a few years before Shakespeare had fully developed as a writer) had changed the face of drama. They were one-man plays —"star vehicles," as they might be called today— built around one central figure. It is hardly too much to say that Marlowe wrote his plays in this way because the great Edward Alleyn, who was well over six feet tall and possessed of a tremendously powerful voice, was on hand to take the leading roles in them. For several years Marlowe and Alleyn helped the Admiral's Men to keep their place as the second most popular company in London. The only group that was more popular was the Chamberlain's Men, who could boast Shakespeare the writer, and Burbage the actor.

Richard Burbage was Alleyn's chief rival for the title of "the greatest actor of the day." Born about 1573, he started to act while he was still a child, and he may have gained experience by performing, on tour in the country, the parts that Alleyn acted in London. By the time he was twenty-one, Burbage was a full-fledged member of the Chamberlain's Men. He is said to have had a quality of personal magnetism that radiated from the stage and enthralled his audiences. Of the two men, Alleyn may have been the more forceful, Burbage, the more subtle. At the same time, it must be remembered that a large measure of Burbage's success was due to the parts that he was given to play. He was very probably the first Prince Hal, the first Henry V, the first Hamlet, the first Othello, Mark Antony, and Prospero—to name but a few. (It is interesting that as both Shakespeare and Burbage aged, the heroes of many of the plays that Shakespeare wrote tended to be older and older men. Prince Hal is twenty-two. Burbage himself was not much older than that when he played the part for the first time, about 1598. Hamlet is thirty. Othello and Mark Antony—in *Antony and Cleopatra*—are both over thirty-five, and Prospero is over forty-five.) Burbage died in 1619. At his death, some people felt moved to say that Hamlet and Othello, and other characters, too, had died with him. Time has proved that fear to have been ill-founded, but it was, nevertheless, a sincere and well-meant tribute to an exceptional actor.

Burbage was certainly the greatest of the actors among the Chamberlain's Men but he was not the only one of ability or with a great popular following. There was Will Kempe, the comedian, whom Shakespeare undoubtedly had in mind when he wrote the parts of Peter in *Romeo and Juliet,* of Bottom in *A Midsummer Night's Dream,* and of Dogberry in *Much Ado About Nothing.* Kempe quit the company about 1599, and his place was taken by Robert Armin, evidently an even better actor than Kempe, or, in any case, one less given to slapstick comedy. For Armin, Shakespeare probably wrote the part of Feste in *Twelfth Night,* and, above all, the great part of the Fool in *King Lear.* Other actors included Thomas Pope, who may have been the first Falstaff, the first Toby Belch, and the first Shylock. There was William Sly, who may have done Hotspur and Laertes. Augustine Phillips, who evidently had a "lean and hungry" look, could have played Cassius, Malvolio, and Claudius. And there was Shakespeare himself.

Tradition says that Shakespeare played, among other parts, Adam in *As You Like It*, and the Ghost of Hamlet's father. It is just possible that he also did the part of King Lear on at least one occasion. We really know very little of his ability as an actor. He is said to have been "a handsome, well-shaped man," and good looks have always been an asset to an actor. At the same time, there is reason to think that he was soft-spoken, reserved, and retiring by nature. Elizabethan actors had to have loud voices, if they were to be heard by four or five thousand people in theaters that were open to the air, and extrovert natures, because they were not infrequently heckled by the spectators. Shakespeare was probably a good actor, but not a brilliant one. It is also probable that he became an actor, and continued to act (which he certainly did until at least 1603) partly in order to become thoroughly familiar with drama from the presentation, rather than from the purely literary, point of view. Shakespeare's plays are great poetry, but they are also great theater. When they are performed well, they are exciting, fast-moving, funny, and heart-wrenching. Certainly Elizabethan Londoners found them so; otherwise Shakespeare could not, in a highly competitive field, have kept his place as the most popular of playwrights for more than a quarter of a century.

The first plays that Shakespeare wrote were the three parts of *Henry VI* (in 1590 and 1591), *Richard III,* and *Titus Andronicus* (1592). All five were clearly influenced by the spirit of nationalism that ran through England after the defeat of the Spanish Armada; and they were also influenced by the tumultuous plays of Christopher Marlowe. All five were very popular with the playgoers, but only *Richard III* has kept its popularity down to today. The other four are now considered among Shakespeare's least successful works.

Perhaps Shakespeare himself was somewhat dissatisfied with what he had written. In 1593, he turned to comedy and produced *The Comedy of Errors* and *The Taming of the Shrew,* and, in 1594, *The Two Gentlemen of Verona* and *Love's Labour's Lost.* But in 1595 and 1596, trouble with Spain flared up again, and Shakespeare returned to English history, producing his great historical plays: *Richard II* in 1595; *King John* in 1596; the two parts of *Henry IV* in 1597 and 1598; and finally, *Henry V* in 1599. He also wrote *Romeo and Juliet* in 1595. 1595 was thus his first year of unqualified greatness as a dramatist. If he had suddenly ceased to write after he had produced *Richard II* and *Romeo and Juliet,* his name would still be inscribed in history among those of the immortals.

Richard II is a tragedy as much as it is a history play. Shakespeare used poetic license to change some of the facts of the reign of King Richard II (king of England from 1377 to 1399), and also to rework the character of the king himself, in order to suit his dra-

matic needs. He tells the tale of a man who is a bad
king, but a fine person; and yet this king believes
himself to be—and is believed by many of his subjects
to be—king of England by divine right. Even if he is
a weak and ineffectual monarch, has anyone in the
nation the moral or legal right to unseat him from his
God-given throne?

> Not all the water in the rough rude sea
> Can wash the balm from an anointed king;
> The breath of worldly men cannot depose
> The deputy elected by the Lord.

But Henry Bolingbroke, Richard's cousin, is angered
by the fact that the king has banished him, and has
confiscated his father's property. He returns to England from banishment, and raises civil war. Richard,
although he continues to believe in the divine right of
kings, is at once so wise and so weak a person that he
bows before the storm (Act III):

> For God's sake, let us sit upon the ground
> And tell sad stories of the death of kings:
> How some have been depos'd, some slain in war,
> Some haunted by the ghosts they have depos'd,
> Some poison'd by their wives, some sleeping
>   killed;
> All murder'd: for within the hollow crown
> That rounds the mortal temples of a king
> Keeps Death his court, and there the antick sits,
> Scoffing his state and grinning at his pomp;
> Allowing him a breath, a little scene,

To monarchize, be fear'd, and kill with looks,
Infusing him with self and vain conceit
As if this flesh which walls about our life
Were brass impregnable; and humour'd thus
Comes at the last, and with a little pin
Bores through his castle wall, and farewell king!

He is deposed, imprisoned, and murdered. Henry Bolingbroke becomes king.

One of Shakespeare's triumphs in *Richard II* is the poetry that he puts into the mouth of Henry's father, John of Gaunt. Shakespeare's John of Gaunt and the John of Gaunt of history are two very different persons. Yet such was Shakespeare's ability as a poet and as a creator of character, that the pathetic but vigorous old man in the play has become, in the minds of many, the real John of Gaunt. Nor is it any wonder that this is so, when he is given lines such as the following to speak (Act I, Scene iii):

> For, ere the six years that he hath to spend
> Can change their moons and bring their times
>   about,
> My oil-dried lamp and time-bewasted light
> Shall be extinct with age and endless night;
> My inch of taper will be burnt and done,
> And blindfold death not let me see my son.

The Henry Bolingbroke of *Richard II* is King Henry IV in the two parts of *Henry IV*. *Richard II* had been a history play laced with tragedy. Both parts of *Henry*

44

IV are history plays laced with comedy. The comedy, the humor, the laughter are provided by the mountainous figure of Sir John Falstaff that

> . . . huge hill of flesh . . . [that] tun of a man . . . that trunk of humours . . . that bolting-hutch of beastliness, that swollen parcel of dropsies, that huge bombard of sack, that stuffed cloak-bag of guts . . .

Falstaff is one of Shakespeare's great creations. Any person asked to name the three or four most outstanding figures that Shakespeare ever produced would surely list Falstaff as one of them.

The thing about Falstaff is that he has no visible virtues. He is a drunkard, a glutton, a liar, a thief, perhaps even a coward, and certainly, as far as his great girth and advancing years will permit, a pursuer of women. For all of that, he is one of the most amiable characters in literature. It is impossible to dislike him, and it is also impossible to say why we like him. Reason and logic say that Falstaff is a sink of iniquity. He is the Lord of Misrule. Although he is neither vicious nor brutal, he is the human incarnation of all that is deplorable in "the world, the flesh, and the Devil." Still, our emotions say that we like him, although we cannot explain why. Perhaps this is because art cannot be explained logically, for art is, in one sense, the triumph of heart over head, of feelings over logic. Falstaff is a masterpiece of art.

Falstaff even goes so far as to attack the virtue that most men, down through the centuries, have always prized more highly than any other—honor itself:

45

Can honour set to a leg? No. Or an arm? No. Or take away the grief of a wound? No. Honour hath no skill in surgery then? No. What is honour? A word. What is that word, honour? Air. A trim reckoning! Who hath it? He that died o' Wednesday. Doth he feel it? No. Doth he hear it? No. It is insensible then? Yea, to the dead. But will it not live with the living? No. Why? Detraction will not suffer it. Therefore I'll none of it: honour is a mere scutcheon; and so ends my catechism.

The Elizabethan audiences loved Falstaff. He was such a favorite with Queen Elizabeth that, according to tradition, she commanded Shakespeare to write a third play, one that would show Falstaff in love. Shakespeare, of course, acted on the royal command and after two weeks had written *The Merry Wives of Windsor*. The play is funny. Falstaff in it is still fat and badly behaved. Somehow, though, he is not the same Falstaff. The true Falstaff, the exquisite sinner, is really found only in *Henry IV, Part One*.

In the two parts of *Henry IV*, Shakespeare again availed himself of poetic license and altered history considerably. He made Falstaff and Prince Hal, the heir to the throne, bosom friends and companions in mischief. But Falstaff, as Shakespeare presents him, never existed. (Shakespeare had originally given the name of Oldcastle to the character. The descendants of the real Sir John Oldcastle quite properly protested, and Shakespeare was obliged to look for another name. He dipped into the cast of characters of

Henry VI, Part One, took the name of Sir John Fastolfe, and altered it slightly. This time, the descendants of the real Fastolfe protested, but the name remained.) Prince Hal was, perhaps, in real life not quite the wild young man that Shakespeare pictured him to be, although legends about his somewhat indecorous youth had started to circulate before Shakespeare had begun to write his plays. It was, however, to Shakespeare's purpose to create a disreputable Falstaff and a hot-blooded heir to the throne. The theme of the play lies just beneath the surface in *Henry IV*: it is the education of a king. Since Prince Hal, as King Henry V, became a hero-king, beloved and respected by his people, we must assume that his education had been sound. The most painful and difficult thing he had to learn was how to disentangle himself from Falstaff—that is, to disentangle himself from all the irresponsible merriment that Falstaff represented. Thus at the end of *Henry IV, Part Two*, just after Prince Hal has been crowned, we read:

Falstaff.   God save thee, my sweet boy! ...
King Henry V.   I know thee not, old man:
                 fall to thy prayers;
    How ill white hairs become a fool and jester!
    I have long dream'd of such a kind of man,
    So surfeit-swell'd, so old and so profane;
    But, being awak'd, I do despise my dream.

This is a sacrifice that a king—a responsible and effectual chief of state—must make. He must practice discipline, chiefly of himself. He must keep himself from the sensual pleasures of the world. He must study courage and impartiality. If he does not do these things, he will be (like Richard II) a fine man perhaps, but a bad king. Shakespeare does not say that discipline, courage, and unworldliness are noble, moral, and desirable for all of us. He simply lets us see how lonely and how difficult the life of a good king, a "working monarch," must be.

For much of the time between May, 1592, and May, 1594, the plague kept the theaters closed near London. Therefore, Strange's Men toured the country districts of England, visiting Cambridge, Oxford, Gloucester, and Coventry. Shakespeare may have gone with them, or he may have returned to Stratford. Wherever he was, it was at this time that he wrote *Venus and Adonis* and *The Rape of Lucrece.*

During the months in which the theaters were allowed to operate in London, Strange's Men performed at the Rose. Built about 1587, the Rose was a Bankside theater; that is, it was in the part of London that lay across the Thames from St. Paul's and the Tower, and from the Theatre and the Curtain. Some of this part of London, too, was a liberty, outside the jurisdiction of the city authorities, and it became the entertainment quarter of the area. At one time there were four Bankside theaters (the Rose, the Swan, the Globe, and the Hope); and there were also Bankside bull-and-bear-baiting gardens, as well as bars and taverns of varying degrees of disrepute. Shakespeare's plays did not start life in the "nice zones" of the city.

Shakespeare had become famous, despite the fact that his plays were being put on in the slums; despite the fact that for about two years, right at the opening of his career, his plays could not have a London performance at all; and despite the fact, too, that he was still a young man (only thirty years old in 1594). In fact, he had had a meteoric rise to fame. Because he lived so long ago and, partly, because we study Shakespeare's plays today in school, as well as see them on the stage or in films, we tend to think of Shakespeare as a remote, scholarly, permanently middle-aged man, with a beard and a very sober outlook on life. But it is highly unlikely that he was that way at all.

Shakespeare started his career as a bright young man, though personally he was perhaps retiring and even shy. Certainly he was very much involved in the brawling, lively, colorful life of his day. His plays are full of indirect references to, and "in jokes" about, people and events of his own time. Many of his scenes are crowd scenes, and many are built around duels, battles, murders, and other forms of violence, all of which were acted out with shocking realism on the stage. (For example, in Shakespeare's day, if one actor was to "kill" another in a stage fight, the one to be killed wore a pouch of goat's blood under his costume. When he was stabbed, the blood would gush out all over the stage in a hideously lifelike way, and to the great delight of the spectators.) Shakespeare was often bawdy, too, and not at all above putting any number of off-color jokes into his text. He was, in a word, a crowd-pleaser. The surfaces of his plays were intended to

49

delight the groundlings. Shakespeare was a working man of the theater, who wrote with his finger on the pulse of the audience of the day. He made sure that the spectators got what they liked. He also—and in this ability lay much of his genius—was able to mold the taste of the times, and make the spectators like what they got. Subtly and unobtrusively, he refined and made beautiful whatever subject he touched. Every play that Shakespeare wrote has, not far below the sparkling, crowd-pleasing surface, themes and ideas of great and permanent importance. The insides, as it were, of his plays are always made up of beauty, wisdom, and truth.

At this time, as Shakespeare was enjoying the sensation of having suddenly become one of the most popular writers of England, two things happened that must have plunged him into worry and sadness. The first was that the town of Stratford was nearly destroyed by fire. In 1594 and 1595, in two of the disastrous fires that so often consumed whole villages and cities before the advent of running water and of fire brigades, over two hundred buildings in Stratford were gutted, and nearly half of the inhabitants were left without homes. And in August, 1596, little Hamnet Shakespeare, just eleven years old, died and was buried in the Stratford churchyard. Shakespeare had lost his only son.

5. The Comedies

In Act III of *King John*, Constance, in anguish for her son Arthur, speaks these lines:

> Grief fills the room up of my absent child,
> Lies in his bed, walks up and down with me,
> Puts on his pretty looks, repeats his words,
> Remembers me of all his gracious parts,
> Stuffs out his vacant garments with his form:
> Then have I reason to be fond of grief.
> Fare you well: had you such a loss as I,
> I could give better comfort than you do.

Is this only the voice of Constance? Or can we hear in these words the voice of Shakespeare himself? Is this not really Shakespeare's own sorrow for the death of his son?

Scholars and critics are not at all in agreement about whether or not Shakespeare, in writing his plays, consciously drew from events in his own life. If he did

51

not draw consciously from his own life, did he do it unconsciously? Could Shakespeare, for example, have expressed true grief for the death of a child, if he himself had not experienced grief for the death of his own?

To attempt any answer at all to this question, it is necessary to establish the date of (in this particular case) *King John*. If Constance's lines were written before August, 1596, then obviously they could not contain any reference to the death of Hamnet. If, however, they were written after August, 1596, they may well have been written with Hamnet in mind.

It is not an easy thing to establish exactly the date of any Shakespearian play. Unfortunately, neither he nor any of his family or friends left any diaries or letters that mention his work. The only date known for certain about *King John* is that it had been written before the end of 1598. In September of that year, a man named Francis Meres wrote a book in which he mentioned the play "King Iohn," by Shakespeare. Thus Constance's lines could have been written after Hamnet's death, but there is no sure evidence to prove that they were.

Many of Shakespeare's plays do contain indirect and slightly veiled references to current events and to people famous in his day. He refers, for instance, to Christopher Marlowe, and to a series of sixteenth-century Puritan articles signed "Martin Marprelate," in *As You Like It*. He refers to the Earl of Essex' expedition of 1599 to Ireland in *Henry V*. He discusses Elizabethan acting techniques in *Hamlet*. Yet if Shakespeare was able to express grief convincingly over the death of a child only because his own son had died, what is to be said, then, about the horror that Macbeth and his wife feel for having murdered Duncan? It would be ridiculous to argue that Shakespeare had committed murder, too, since he wrote about it so effectively.

The question is really one of the nature and of the power of artistic imagination. Could Shakespeare, or can anyone, understand truth only through experience? Is it possible to know the true nature of things through imagination alone? Must a person know pain himself before he can understand someone else's pain? To speak intelligently of love, must someone have been in love himself? And are the sensations that he feels the same sensations as any other person's? Shakespeare said something on this subject at the beginning of Act V of *A Midsummer Night's Dream*, a play he probably wrote about the time that he wrote *King John*.

> Lovers and madmen have such seething brains,
> Such shaping fantasies, that apprehend
> More than cool reason ever comprehends.
> The lunatic, the lover, and the poet,
> Are of imagination all compact:
> One sees more devils than vast hell can hold,
> That is, the madman; the lover, all as frantic,
> Sees Helen's beauty in a brow of Egypt:
> The poet's eye, in a fine frenzy rolling,
> Doth glance from heaven to earth, from earth to
>   heaven;

And, as imagination bodies forth
The forms of things unknown, the poet's pen
Turns them to shapes, and gives to airy nothing
A local habitation and a name.
Such tricks hath strong imagination,
That, if it would apprehend some joy,
It comprehends some bringer of that joy;
Or in the night, imagining some fear,
How easy is a bush suppos'd a bear!

Probably, if we are to believe these lines, Shakespeare was well able to describe accurately sensations that other people feel, but that he himself had perhaps never felt outside of his own imagination. Shakespeare's true greatness seems to lie, not in his ability to describe with exactness the sights that he himself had seen, but in the range, the vividness, and the accuracy of his creative imagination.

On May 4, 1597, Shakespeare bought New Place, the second largest house in Stratford. If nothing else proves that he had become a popular playwright, this transaction alone is convincing. He paid £60 for the property, or what would be about $5,500 now. (In Shakespeare's time £1 bought about what £30 buy today.) Ironically, the sale was attended by a highly dramatic incident. William Underhill, who sold the house to Shakespeare, was murdered by his own son soon after the sale had been completed. The son was executed for the crime early in 1599.

Shakespeare was now a prosperous young landowner in Stratford. New Place had two barns, two gardens, and two orchards. It stood (it was torn down about 1760) just two blocks from the house on Henley Street where he had been born. Undoubtedly, Shakespeare moved his wife and two daughters into New Place, and perhaps invited his mother and father to share it with them, too. Since Stratford was only a two-day journey from London, perhaps Shakespeare became a sort of commuter between the city and his home. He would go to London for a month, four or five times a year, when he was acting in a play or seeing one of his own through rehearsal; and he would return to Stratford to write and to be with his family during the rest of the year.

Between 1595 and 1600, Shakespeare wrote not only his great history plays, but also his great comedies. His first had been *A Comedy of Errors* in 1593. In 1594, came *Love's Labour's Lost*, the first of his pieces for the theater to be published with his name on the title page.

Love's Labour's Lost is a strange play of talk, jokes, and puns—the full meaning of which may have been entirely topical, and so may be lost to us today. In the play, four young men decide to take an oath to withdraw from the world in order to study and to acquire wisdom, and, for three years, to avoid the company of all women. They soon recognize the folly of this vow when several young ladies, eager for attention, turn up in the vicinity of their scholarly retreat. Learning divorced from love cannot, they decide, be worthwhile or true. This sentiment is expressed in Act IV by

Berowne, who some people think is a partial portrait by Shakespeare of himself.

> Now, for not looking on a woman's face,
> You have in that forsworn the use of eyes . . .
> O! we have made a vow to study, Lords,
> And in that vow we have forsworn our books:
> For when would you, my liege, or you, or you,
> In leaden contemplation have found out
> Such fiery numbers as the prompting eyes
> Of beauty's tutors have enrich'd you with? . . .
> But love first learned in a lady's eyes,
> Lives not alone immured in the brain,
> But, with the motion of all elements,
> Courses as swift as thought in every power,
> And gives to every power a double power,
> Above their functions and their offices.
> It adds a precious seeing to the eye;
> A lover's eyes will gaze an eagle blind . . .
> And when Love speaks, the voice of all the gods
> Makes heaven drowsy with the harmony.
> Never durst poet touch a pen to write
> Until his ink were temper'd with Love's
>   sighs . . .

Love's Labour's Lost is not entirely a light or a funny play. As in nearly all of Shakespeare's comedies, side by side with the fun, there is a vein of seriousness, of perplexity, even of sadness. In this one, a grave moment is provided by Holofernes, the awkward, clumsy, talkative schoolmaster. He takes part in a sketch (in 1594, Shakespeare was already making use of the idea of a play within a play) in which he acts the part of Judas. But the people that watch his act jeer his efforts, and laugh at him. Holofernes, much offended, replies to them. Suddenly the whole comedy atmosphere is interrupted:

This is not generous, not gentle, not humble

and he stumbles sadly off the stage.

About two years after Shakespeare had completed *Love's Labour's Lost*, he wrote *A Midsummer Night's Dream*. This is the airiest and the lightest of his plays, a piece of whimsy and fantasy, abounding in love potions, transformations, and magic songs. It is also one of the most difficult of the Shakespearian plays to stage. Directors in the twentieth century have adopted such techniques as covering half of the actors in gold paint, or of populating the stage with live rabbits, in attempts to provide a background of substance, a "local habitation" for Shakespeare's "airy nothing."

It was, however, the composer Felix Mendelssohn, rather than any actor or director, that seems to have best understood Shakespeare's mood and intentions in this comedy. In 1826, when Mendelssohn was only seventeen years old, he wrote an overture to *A Midsummer Night's Dream*, and several years later some other pieces of incidental music (including the famous "Wedding March") that are an exquisite comment on the play. Inevitably, many of Shakespeare's plays have attracted the attention and the efforts of composers. Ambroise Thomas made an opera of *Hamlet*. Henry Purcell provided music for a seventeenth-century version of *The Tempest*. Giuseppe Verdi wrote an opera based on *Macbeth*, and late in life, two brilliant and beautiful operas based on *Othello* and *The Merry Wives of Windsor*. But perhaps Mendelssohn, more than anyone else, was the musician who proved able to put into music the spirit and the genius of a Shakespeare play.

About 1596, Shakespeare wrote a comedy that has since been lost. Its title was *Love's Labour's Won*. That it existed is known first of all from the book called *Palladis Tamia: Wit's Treasury*, published in 1598 by Francis Meres. Meres wrote in his book that Shakespeare was "the most excellent writer" in English of both comedy and tragedy. He also said that Shakespeare was "the most passionate among us to bewail and bemoan the perplexities of love." To substantiate his opinions, Meres gives a list of the twelve plays by Shakespeare with which he was evidently familiar. Among them is *Love's Labour's Won*. It has often been said that Meres made a mistake, and either that no such play ever existed, or that *Love's Labour's Won* was merely an alternative title for *The Taming of the Shrew,* or for an early version of *Much Ado About Nothing*. An inventory, however, was recently discovered that was drawn up in 1603 by Christopher Hunt, a bookseller in the city of Exeter. Hunt lists *The Taming of the Shrew*, *Love's Labour's Lost*, and *Love's Labour's Won* among the books that he had on hand. So it may well, indeed, have been a separate play, written, performed, and published. Why the text of it vanished, and whether a copy of it exists anywhere on earth, are interesting questions. The more romantic scholars hope that the attic of some old country house, or a trunk that has been gathering dust for two centuries in some forgotten barn, will one day yield up *Love's Labour's Won.* It is probably a forlorn hope. The more sober scholars reject it. If, however, the play should appear, the discoverer would be holding in his hands a volume of incalculable value.

In October, 1598, Shakespeare received the only letter written to him that has been preserved. Ironically, it was a request for money, written by a Stratford man named Richard Quiney. Addressing himself to "my loving good friend and countryman, Mr. Wm. Shakespeare," Quiney asks for "your help with thirty pounds"—about $2,750. There is no proof that Shakespeare let Quiney have the money, but from another letter that Quiney wrote to a man named Sturley, it seems that the loan was made. In any case, it is hardly likely that Quiney would have made the request if he had not known that Shakespeare was fairly rich. Success had naturally brought Shakespeare money. It had also begun to attract around him, evidently, people who usually flock about those that have made money, to pester them for their "help and understanding."

After the death of Hamnet and the purchase of New Place, during the time of his newly acquired financial security and an increasing burden of work, Shakespeare continued to write comedies. The years 1599 and 1600 saw him produce *As You Like It* and *Twelfth Night.*

In *As You Like It,* Shakespeare builds his play

around one of his favorite themes: love at first sight. Rosalind and Orlando no sooner lay eyes on each other than they fall in love. Celia as quickly falls in love with Oliver. Love is blind, so tradition says, and so it said to Shakespeare. Was this love at first sight true love or only infatuation? Rosalind, Celia, Orlando, and Oliver retire to the Forest of Arden. Rosalind disguises herself as a boy and tries to argue Orlando out of his devotion, to persuade him that he is not in love at all. She fails in her attempt, and wins a husband. Love at first sight, in *As You Like It* anyway, is true love.

As You Like It is a comedy of youth and of the heart. At the opening of the play, the young lovers are caught in a web of turmoils and deceits spun by their elders. They go into the Forest of Arden, an almost magical country, a sort of imaginary Garden of Eden, where people can live virtually untroubled by "the way of the world." It is in this "serene and blessed" place that love can flourish. No one is called on to wrestle there with the evils and dishonesty of society. People need only to follow the urgings of the heart. Yet in the forest, away from their elders, away from the pressures of discipline, the young lovers do not live a disordered or an immoral life. They replace the commands of the outside world with honest compulsions from within themselves. The emphasis here may be placed legitimately on the word "honest." Shakespeare at no time preaches to his readers or to his audience. He never instructs, threatens, or cajoles. He advocates no particular religious faith, philosophy, or code of ethics. Even so, we cannot fail to notice in many of his plays how often good grows out of honesty, and how often evil comes from dishonesty.

Two of the most interesting characters in *As You Like It* are Touchstone and Jaques. (Adam would be the most interesting of all if we could be sure that, as is said, Shakespeare himself acted the part, and therefore may have written it with himself in mind.) Touchstone was the first of Shakespeare's great clowns. The part was probably written for Robert Armin, after Will Kempe had left the Chamberlain's Men. Kempe was evidently an able actor, but also a self-centered and extravagant one. His idea of a good show was to dance—not walk—from London to Norwich, an exploit that took him a month in the year 1600. (It is also said that in 1601 he danced his way over the Alps. If he actually did, it seems obvious that the man was a study in misspent energy. In Kempe's defense, however, it must be conceded that many people of the fifteenth, sixteenth, and seventeenth centuries engaged in one form or another of "marathon dancing." They did so, in most cases, because they believed that dancing was an effective safeguard against the plague.)

Robert Armin was a more subtle and a more tender man. For him, Shakespeare was able to write confidently the most paradoxical and the most difficult parts that he ever composed: Touchstone, Feste (in *Twelfth Night*), and, above all, the Fool in *King Lear*.

These three remarkable characters "are not altogether fool." In their puns, their jokes, their nonsense, and their songs, they give expression to some of the greatest wisdom that any of the plays contain. In real life, the fool, the court jester, had been

61

traditionally an illiterate, perhaps half-demented man, whose only accomplishments were an ability to sing songs in a cracked voice, to make jokes, and to turn somersaults. He was to be laughed at, but never to be listened to. Were Shakespeare's three great fools perhaps, in some way, a defense of himself and of theater in general? After all, Shakespeare was, and many of the actors and dramatists of the day were, men who had had little formal education, who were expected by nobles and groundlings alike to be acrobats and entertainers, but little more. The theater in 1600 occupied the same relative position in London as that occupied by the fool in legendary royal palaces. Yet Shakespeare knew that he had something more to offer than simply a colorful superficial show. He knew that in spite of his not having attended a university, in spite of his not having been of noble birth, what he was writing was more than just puns and jigs and somersaults. In one of his sonnets, he says as much:

Not marble, nor the gilded monuments
Of princes, shall outlive this powerful rhyme . . .

Perhaps Shakespeare's great fools were created by him to be, in part, his own subtle advocates.

On the other hand, Jaques, in *As You Like It*, is not a fool but a man of melancholy. (Shakespeare's greatest man of melancholy is Hamlet, whom he created two years after he had written *As You Like It*.) "Melancholy" today is a word that suggests gloominess and sadness, a downcast mood that may pass in an hour or in a day or in a very few days at most. In

Shakespeare's time, melancholy meant something different. It was a condition in which a person alternated between great joy and angry sorrow; in which a person took very seriously everything that was said to him; and in which he often had troublesome, bad dreams. Several writers and thinkers on human behavior in Elizabethan England (they were not called psychologists then) wrote at length on melancholy. One of these was Timothy Bright, a man who also devised one of the first systems of shorthand. Shakespeare had surely either read, or had heard discussed, Bright's *Treatise of Melancholie.*

Neither Jaques nor Hamlet is only and entirely a man of melancholy. Neither is a sick or a deranged man. Shakespeare did not ever write a play about people who were irrational, or who might have been cured by a doctor. None of his characters are clinical cases. At the same time, both Jaques and Hamlet are to a certain extent melancholy—perhaps to the extent that a man may be thought of as only sulky rather than bad-tempered. Jaques is described as having been so troubled when he saw a deer that hunters had wounded that he began to reflect gloomily on the fact that man must attack and kill animals in order to eat. And it is Jaques that speaks some of Shakespeare's most famous lines, those describing life as a silly and even somewhat bitter process (Act II, Scene vii):

All the world's a stage
And all the men and women merely players:
They have their exits and their entrances;
And one man in his time plays many parts,

His acts being seven ages. At first the infant,
Mewling and puking in the nurse's arms.
And then the whining schoolboy, with his satchel,
And shining morning face, creeping like snail
Unwillingly to school. And then the lover,
Sighing like furnace, with a woeful ballad
Made to his mistress' eyebrow. Then a soldier,
Full of strange oaths, and bearded like the pard,
Jealous in honour, sudden and quick in quarrel,
Seeking the bubble reputation
Even in the cannon's mouth. And then the justice,
In fair round belly with good capon lined,
With eyes severe, and beard of formal cut,
Full of wise saws and modern instances;
And so he plays his part. The sixth age shifts
Into the lean and slipper'd pantaloon,
With spectacles on nose and pouch on side,
His youthful hose well sav'd, a world too wide
For his shrunk shank; and his big manly voice
Turning again toward childish treble, pipes
And whistles in his sound. Last scene of all,
That ends this strange eventful history,
Is second childishness and mere oblivion,
Sans teeth, sans eyes, sans taste, sans everything.

The year after writing *As You Like It*, Shakespeare wrote *Twelfth Night*, one of his funniest plays. The basic plot is of a girl named Viola who dresses up as a man in order to get a job at the court of a young nobleman named Orsino. Orsino hires Viola, and immediately sends her off to plead his love before a reluctant lady named Olivia. Olivia falls in love not with Orsino but with Viola, who, dressed up in doublet and hose, cuts a very handsome manish figure. And when Viola's identical twin brother later appears, Olivia, in an access of passion, drags him off to be married before he can so much as open his mouth to question the oddity of a half-minute courtship engineered by a lady. These sparkling mysteries of love are acted out against a background of the drinking, singing, and dancing of a pair of disreputable knights; one a thin fellow named Sir Andrew Aguecheek, and the other a fat chap named Sir Toby Belch. Sir Andrew is among the most simpleminded of all the characters that have ever walked out onto a stage; and Sir Toby is a kind of latter-day Falstaff, whose ambitions do not rise much higher than the foam on a glass of ale.

Mixed with the drinking, the singing, and the muddled love affairs of *Twelfth Night*, is the character of Malvolio. Self-righteous and self-important, he is in contrast to all the fun, the object of the insults and the practical jokes of the roisterers. When he finally understands how much he has been made a fool and a laughingstock by everyone around him, he snarls out his last line in the play:

I'll be revenged on the whole pack of you

and immediately the atmosphere of a comedy has again been electrically interrupted. Holofernes in *Love's Labour's Lost* did it with sorrow and disillusionment; Malvolio does it with bitterness and anger.

65

Something had changed in Shakespeare. After writing *Twelfth Night*, and after creating Sir Toby and Sir Andrew as well as the acid Malvolio, Shakespeare abandoned comedy. He did not ever write another gaily funny play. His own humor became bitter, sometimes sarcastic, as able to provoke tears as well as laughter. Immediately after having completed *Twelfth Night*, he wrote his five great tragedies. He emerged from this tragic period to write the nearly serene romances of *The Winter's Tale* and *The Tempest*. But in spite of what Sir Toby Belch had said, for Shakespeare, the playwright, there were to be no more "cakes and ale."

6. The Tragedies of Queen Elizabeth's Reign

During the year 1598, the Chamberlain's Men performed their plays at the Curtain theater, but they were no longer satisfied with the premises. They also were having difficulties over their rent contract. The "Theatre" was still standing, but the Chamberlain's Men did not want to move into it; it was, after all, nearly twenty-five years old, and no longer large enough for the now famous company. In December of 1598, therefore, Richard Burbage and his brother, Cuthbert, made plans to build a new theater for the Chamberlain's Men. They decided to save money by pulling down the Theatre, which to all intents and purposes they owned. They used the wood in the construction of a new theater on the south bank of the Thames, near the Rose and the Swan.

On December 28, 1598, a carpenter named Peter

Street, along with several helpers, began dismantling the Theatre and trundling the boards and planks through the streets of London, across London Bridge, to a site on Maiden Lane just opposite the Rose. Undoubtedly, Shakespeare himself spent part of the winter of 1598–99 carrying loads of lumber, and helping in the construction of the new building. Inevitably, the Chamberlain's Men were sued by the man who still owned the land on which the Theatre stood, because they "did . . . in most forcible and ryotous manner take and carry away from thence all the wood and timber." The Burbages won the case.

By September, 1599, the new theater had been completed and was ready for occupancy. It was named the Globe. It was to be the theater in which Shakespeare's greatest tragedies would be first performed.

While Shakespeare was briefly working as a wrecker and carpenter, and at the same time writing a tragedy to be performed when the Globe was ready, a real-life tragedy was being acted out in England. It involved the Earl of Essex, the brilliant and handsome friend of the Earl of Southampton, and the favorite of Queen Elizabeth.

Essex was thirty-three years old in 1599. He was respected by his friends and idolized by the people. No man in the country seemed to have a more brilliant career before him. But his fame and success went to his head. In March, 1599, Queen Elizabeth sent him to Ireland to crush a rebellion that had been raised by the Earl of Tyrone. Essex did not crush the rebellion. Instead, he made a truce with Tyrone and came back

—almost fled back—to London, in September, 1599. Elizabeth was, understandably, much displeased, and Essex realized that the Irish expedition had all but ruined his once promising career. Unwisely, he decided to try to save his fortunes by turning rebel himself. On February 8, 1601, he marched at the head of three hundred men (Southampton among them) into the heart of London, declaring that he wanted to "liberate" the Queen from her evil ministers. What he meant by this was that he wanted to overthrow the Queen. But Essex had overestimated his popularity. Although the people of London loved him, they loved Elizabeth more. Not one Londoner joined the rebellious group of three hundred, and Essex was quickly captured. He was tried on February 19. Even his old friend Francis Bacon deserted him and spoke against him. Elizabeth was brokenhearted, for Essex had been a gentleman upon whom she had "built an absolute trust." He was beheaded on February 25, 1601.

The story of the fall of Essex is a tragedy as the word "tragedy" has most often been defined. Essex was a man who occupied a high place, and who fell to disgrace and death. His fall was brought about, not by the intrigues of his enemies, nor by the workings of chance, but as a result of his own character and actions. Essex was ambitious, charming, handsome, brave, and intelligent. He was also vain and petulant, and not quite as intelligent as he thought that he was. His virtues had raised him, while he was still young, to a pinnacle of fame and prestige, but he wanted even more. His defects of character urged him to try to seize power that had not been conferred on him. His petulancy made him see Queen Elizabeth's reproofs (after he had returned from Ireland, she went so far as to box him on the ear) as more severe than they were. His vanity led him to imagine that all Englishmen would flock to any cause that he led. His intelligence failed to inform him of how to plot and carry out a subtle and effective rebellion. Essex' fall was due to the collapse of his own character. After his trial, he was appropriately penitent; but his penitence came too late.

Shakespeare played a singular part in this abortive rebellion. It might even have turned out to have been a dangerous part. On Friday, February 6, 1601, Sir Charles Percy and Sir Jocelyn Percy, two members of Essex' band, went to the Globe to ask that a special performance of *Richard II* be given the next day. The Chamberlain's Men at first refused; but when they were offered two pounds over their regular profits, they agreed to put the play on. Certainly none of the actors knew that Essex was plotting the overthrow of Queen Elizabeth. If they had, they would not have been persuaded to put on this play, with its tale of the overthrow of an English king, at any price.

On Saturday, February 7, many of Essex' friends came to the Globe to watch the performance. At significant moments they shouted and applauded. A theater was indeed being put to a use that the authorities of London had very much wanted to avoid. It was being used to heat up sedition and rebellion. Inevitably, after Essex had been captured, the Chamberlain's

Men were closely questioned. The authorities wanted to find out just what part they had had in the plot against the queen. The Chamberlain's Men managed to convince their examiners that they were entirely innocent; that they had put on *Richard II* with no evil intentions, but only because several gentlemen had paid for a special performance. They had been as surprised by the violence and the treachery of the next day as anyone in London.

The Chamberlain's Men undoubtedly were innocent. It is, however, not improbable that Shakespeare himself had known something of the plot before it was hatched. Southampton was Essex' right-hand man. Shakespeare had once been, and perhaps still was, a close friend of Southampton's. Was Shakespeare not even slightly suspicious when Southampton's friends requested a special performance of a play about rebellion against a monarch?

Shakespeare must have known that something was in the wind, but he said nothing. Southampton was his friend and his patron, the man who had helped him to get a start in life. There can be little doubt that Shakespeare did not approve of the plans. He did not join the rebellion himself, nor did he write pamphlets or verses directly or covertly in support of the plot. At the same time he admired, or had admired, Essex: there are some lines that refer to him at the opening of Act V of *Henry V*—one of the few times that Shakespeare made an undisguised and direct reference to a living person. Undoubtedly Shakespeare continued to like and to respect Southampton and Essex, but he grew to dislike their cause, and to fear for trouble that it must bring. Then Essex was beheaded. Southampton was sentenced to death, too, but his sentence was commuted to life imprisonment. Shakespeare must have been greatly saddened by the collapse of these two brilliant men. When Queen Elizabeth died two years later, Shakespeare wrote not a single line to honor her memory. He could perhaps not forgive her for having allowed Essex to be executed, and Southampton to be sent to prison.

Shakespeare's greatest tragedies were written between 1600 and 1608. It would be an exaggeration to say that the downfall of Southampton and Essex put him into an eight-year period of gloom and despair in which he would only think bitter thoughts and write grim tragedies. Likewise it would be naïve to believe that he was unaffected by the disgrace into which these two great men had fallen. He had seen a true tragedy acted out before his eyes. He had known the actors in this drama personally. Inevitably, his thoughts turned to the writing of tragedy.

What is a tragedy? A tragedy shows the fall of a great man through his own doings, from a high position down to disgrace and misery and death. Why are tragedies written? A tragedy is an artist's investigation of the nature of life and death.

The writer of tragedy examines the nature of death. He tries to understand why there exists such a phenomenon as death at all. His ultimate intention in dealing with death is to inform himself and his audience about life. If man knew what death was, knew why death was inevitable, why all living things must one day die, perhaps he might understand life better. Perhaps he would be able to lead a more happy and a more peaceful existence.

The writer of tragedy imagines and creates a particular character. He gives that character both emotions and intelligence. He gives him love, jealousy, ambition, fear, generosity, indecision, honesty, cowardice: in short, he tries to make him a true, full, and lifelike figure. He then lets this figure go to a premature death. He lets the ambition or the indecision or jealousy or passion—or still some other quality—dominate the character's life. He shows that this quality can bring a man to suicide or can cause him to be killed. If the character had not allowed the quality to become excessive and dominant, he might have lived to a peaceful old age. But since it does become excessive and dominant, the character is cut down before his time, and suffers a violent death. As we read a tragedy, or watch it performed, we study the causes of the death of its principal character. We try to understand why that character, who possesses those particular qualities, must die prematurely. We then may be able to understand why all men, whatever their qualities and characteristics, must sooner or later die. If we could understand the causes of suicide and violent death, we might learn something about the reasons for the existence of natural death.

Although Shakespeare, both as a man and as a poet, was deeply affected by the fall of Essex, he had written several tragedies before 1601. In 1595, he produced

Romeo and Juliet, one of the most famous plays ever written. It contains some of Shakespeare's most beautiful lines. The names of Romeo and Juliet have become symbols all over the world of young love. Although exquisite and moving, *Romeo and Juliet* is perhaps not among Shakespeare's most profound tragedies. In the prologue to the play, Romeo and Juliet are spoken of as "star-crossed lovers," which is to say, persons caught in a web of destiny, chance, and accident. Indeed, both Romeo and Juliet die as the result of an accident, largely because a message had miscarried. It is impossible to trace a straight line from the characters of Romeo and Juliet to their premature deaths. Both of them were, perhaps, foolish, reckless, and ill-advised in some of their behavior, but their deaths were as much due to accident as to the workings of their characters. We are moved and touched by the sad story that Shakespeare tells us in *Romeo and Juliet,* but in some of his later plays, he was to take his audiences closer to the mystery of life and death.

In 1597, Shakespeare produced *The Merchant of Venice.* This play is usually referred to as a comedy. Technically—because there is a happy ending for the main characters—it is not a tragedy. *The Merchant of Venice,* however, contains the most profound and most intricate character, and also the most tragic one, that Shakespeare had created up to that time. That character is Shylock, a man for whom, in the course of the play, we sometimes feel hatred and sometimes infinite pity.

Shylock lends a large sum of money to Antonio, but only on the condition that if the money is not repaid on the day agreed, he will be allowed to take, in its place, a pound of Antonio's flesh. The agreement seems a silly one to Antonio and to his friend Bassanio, but it is signed. In any case, Antonio knows very well that he will be able to repay the money. But the unexpected happens. The day comes when the debt is due, and Antonio cannot pay. Shylock had not been joking. He goes to court to demand his pound of flesh, willing to show no mercy. But Bassanio's wife, Portia, and Antonio's friends by a series of tricks manage to deprive Shylock of his rightful bargain. In their turn, they show little mercy to Shylock, depriving him of much of his wealth and of his standing in the city of Venice.

The story of Shylock is both complicated and sad. Some critics have at times accused Shakespeare, in this play, of having been anti-Semitic because Shylock is a Jew. But if Shakespeare was anti-Semitic because Shylock drives a hard bargain and is a Jew, then he must have been anti-Scottish because Macbeth was a Scotsman and a murderer; anti-Danish because the king of Denmark in *Hamlet* murdered his own brother; and anti-Italian because, in *The Merchant of Venice*, the court of Venice dispenses merciless and unequal justice to the unfortunate Shylock himself. In truth, Shakespeare was not concerned with ethnic or religious groups. He was interested in individual character, not in race. Shakespeare created in Shylock a rich and merciless man: that he was a Jew was a marginal matter. He created a clever, unscrupulous, and also merciless, woman in Portia; that she was an Italian was also marginal. The point of the play is that Shylock is asked to have mercy on his victim, but he refuses. Then the very persons that had so exalted mercy to Shylock gain the upper hand over him, employing patently illegal means to do so; and they then use toward him neither honesty nor even that very mercy that five minutes before they had talked of in such glowing terms. *The Merchant of Venice* may be technically a comedy. It is, for all of that, a sad and bitter play. In it, Shakespeare gives an unblinking view of the perversity and the cruelty of which men, of whatever religion, are capable.

The play with which the Chamberlain's Men inaugurated their new Globe theater was probably *Julius Caesar*. A doctor from Basel, named Thomas Platter, who was in London in 1599, wrote in an account of his travels that he had seen a play called *Julius Caesar* at a Bankside theater on September 21. Undoubtedly, he was referring to Shakespeare's play.

Julius Caesar has always been one of Shakespeare's most popular works. Generations of schoolchildren have studied it, and have memorized portions of Antony's funeral oration, and have said to each other on all kinds of occasions, "Et tu, Brute!" *Julius Caesar* is also one of Shakespeare's greatest plays. The famous funeral oration is fully deserving of its popularity: it is a triumph of poetry and irony at once; and such lines as

. . . then burst his mighty heart;
And, in his mantle muffling up his face,
Even at the base of Pompey's statue,
Which all the while ran blood, great Caesar fell.
O! what a fall was there, my countrymen;
Then I, and you, and all of us fell down . . .

must surely live as long as the English language itself survives. Shakespeare took the facts of the story
that he tells in *Julius Caesar* from Plutarch's lives of
Brutus and Caesar and Antony, but he stamped the
tale with his own indelible genius. He made the story
of Marcus Brutus into a true tragedy—the first true
tragedy that he had written.

Brutus is a good man: intelligent, brave, unselfish,
and motivated by noble intentions. Yet he is driven
to despair and disgrace, and finally to suicide. It may
seem at first that Brutus was merely the victim of circumstances and of the fortunes of politics and war. At
the beginning we are inclined to agree with Antony's
appraisal of him at the end of Act V:

This was the noblest Roman of them all;
All the conspirators save only he
Did that they did in envy of great Caesar;
He only, in a general honest thought
And common good to all, made one of them.
His life was gentle, and the elements
So mix'd in him that Nature might stand up
And say to all the world, "This was a man!"

Yet, as we read the play, we slowly discover that
perhaps Brutus was not as noble as first he had seemed

77

to be. Antony's words about him are perhaps not to be taken entirely at their face value.

Brutus had, after all, allied himself with a gang of cutthroats and traitors, and had murdered his best friend. He had done this, he said, for the greater good of his country. "Not that I loved Caesar less, but that I loved Rome more." But was Brutus not deluding himself when he spoke these words? For how did he show his great love for Rome? By conspiring against, and murdering, the ruler of the country. But had he, or had any of the conspirators, any idea of how Rome was to be governed after Caesar's death? They had not. Had they prepared to rule Rome themselves? Or had they made plans to call elections or in some way to set up a government to replace the fallen Caesar? They had not. All that they do after killing Caesar is to march up and down the marketplace, waving their swords and shouting, "Peace, Freedom, and Liberty!" Such activities are highly dramatic. They are also highly irresponsible. They court disaster, and in this case disaster was not long in coming. However noble Brutus may have thought his intentions were, what he actually did by killing Caesar was to push his beloved country into anarchy and violence, and to "let slip the dogs of war." Instead of improving the conditions in Rome, Brutus made them worse—and killed his best friend as well.

How could such a noble man make such a hideous mistake? Shakespeare gives a hint of a possible explanation. In the funeral oration that he delivers, Brutus says, doubtless with the utmost sincerity:

... As I slew my best lover for the good of Rome,
I have the same dagger for myself, when it shall
please my country to need my death.

The mob shouts in reply, "Live, Brutus, live! live!"
Yet half an hour later, after Antony has spoken, the
same mob has turned against Brutus: "We'll burn
the house of Brutus." Does Brutus live up to his promise to give his life, as he had taken that of his best
friend, should his fellow Romans demand it? Suddenly, Brutus is not able to honor his words. He and
Cassius ride "like madmen through the gates of
Rome." Brutus cannot be blamed for having fled to
save his life. It was a normal and a natural thing to
do. Yet only a few minutes before, he had been speaking of his honor, and of his readiness to sacrifice his
own life for the good of his country. We are disap-
pointed in Brutus. We are no longer quite so ready to
say that he "was the noblest Roman of them all."

Brutus was not a coward. Rather, he was a reflec-
tive and an intelligent man, who thought himself more
intelligent than in fact he was. In his determination to
assassinate Caesar, he divided the political situation
in Rome into patterns of right and wrong, liberty and
tyranny. He forgot that no social situation, at any
time, is either black or white, but is inevitably some
shade of gray. Brutus was intelligent. His mistake
was that he did not think deeply enough over a long
enough period of time. He forgot that love for, and honesty toward, one's friend are perhaps the noblest of
human qualities—nobler even than love of country.

Mark Antony may have been a self-seeking and over-clever politician to some extent, but above all he is the man who remained loyal to Caesar:

For he was my friend, faithful and just to me . . .

Brutus may seem to be a great and noble man; but in the end, it is Mark Antony that wins the day in Rome, and that probably wins our affections, too.

Shakespeare followed *Julius Caesar* with what was to prove to be his most famous play, and perhaps the single most famous work of literature ever written: the tragedy of *Hamlet, Prince of Denmark.*

It is not surprising that *Hamlet* was written shortly after *Julius Caesar.* Hamlet is, after all, a man whose mental processes are, from one point of view, just the reverse of Brutus'. Brutus does not think long enough or deeply enough. Hamlet thinks "too precisely on the event."

Hamlet's father has just died when the play opens. His ghost returns from the grave to tell Hamlet that he did not die a natural death, but that he had been murdered by his own brother, Claudius. He commands Hamlet to avenge his death. Hamlet vows that he will "with wings as swift as meditation or the thoughts of love . . . sweep to my revenge." But he does not keep this vow. Not only does he not move swiftly to revenge, but he does not ever really accomplish his revenge at all. First he tests the truth of the Ghost's statement. Then he deliberately lets an opportunity go by for killing Claudius. Finally, at the end of the play, he does in fact kill Claudius, but virtually by accident, and as much because Claudius has plotted his death—and seemingly his mother's—as because Claudius had killed his father. Why does Hamlet not sweep to revenge? Why does he not do what he had promised to do? Why does he not act? These questions have perplexed and fascinated people for three centuries, in nearly every country of the world. Millions of words have been spoken and written in an attempt to answer them, but no answer so far seems to be altogether satisfactory.

Hamlet is a tragedy. The hero is Hamlet himself, brought prematurely to death through some aspect of his character. What is that aspect? How does it come about that a noble and intelligent prince, beloved of his people, falls from his high position to a situation in which he is successfully hunted to his death by a criminal wearer of the crown?

Hamlet must not be read as though it were simply a more complicated algebra problem stated in dramatic verse. Neither *Hamlet*, nor any tragedy, can yield a single, neat answer to the problem that it poses. Hamlet himself says that "the end of playing"—which is to say, the purpose of theater—"is to hold, as 'twere, the mirror up to nature." A good play reflects life completely, steadily, and truly. There is no "answer" to a tragedy, any more than there is an answer to life. It is not the tragedian's intention to solve life's problems, but to investigate them. He gives us material that will inspire us and impel us to think about our own lives, about death, and about the world around us. A tragedy is a bright light shone upon life. With our own intelligence and our own poetic perceptions, we come to understand some of the factors in (in this case) the life of Hamlet. We may later examine some of our own behavior in the light of his conduct.

Why does Hamlet not swiftly avenge his father's death, as he said that he would? The explanations for his delay most often given are variations of the statement "because he could not make up his mind." Hamlet has therefore gone down in history as the great hesitator, the great delayer, the great procrastinator. Hamlet delayed so long, thought and considered so much, after having made a decision to act, that, since circumstances changed while he all but stood still, among the deaths that he finally accomplished was his own. It is not difficult to understand that delay and hesitation and procrastination can undo a man. It is wrong to act rashly, thoughtlessly, and carelessly—as Brutus did. Yet it is no less wrong not to execute one's plans and intentions at all. Is it true that Hamlet could not make up his mind?

It used to be argued by some people that Hamlet delayed simply because he went mad. Having learned that his uncle had murdered his father, and having seen his mother marry that uncle, Hamlet's mind, it was thought, became unhinged. "O! what a noble mind is here o'erthrown . . ." says Ophelia, speaking of Hamlet, and some readers have been inclined to agree. It is not, however, probable that Shakespeare had Hamlet go mad, because if Hamlet is mad, if his actions and his lack of them are caused by mental illness,

82

then his story is not a tragedy at all, but only a case history in verse. Poetry is concerned with what is universal and general and permanent. It does not deal chiefly or only with a particular condition of a particular man at a particular time. The reasons why a person might lose his or her mind can be material for a tragedy; but the actual condition of mental instability cannot be.

Hamlet is surely entirely sane. He is, however, to a certain extent a man of melancholy. He alternates quickly between exhilaration and gloom. He thinks and talks at great length about everything that is said to him. It is not, however, his melancholy that prevents him from acting. Melancholy could not do so much. It could color a man's life but it could not change it radically, or destroy it.

And so the question keeps returning: Why did Hamlet not act? Hamlet asks the question, too (IV, iv):

> . . . I do not know
> Why yet I live to say "This thing's to do";
> Sith I have cause and will and strength and means
> To do't . . .

When critics ask of Hamlet "Why did he not act?" they mean "Why did he not kill Claudius?" It is true that Hamlet had made up his mind to murder Claudius —to avenge his father in that way. What is not always remembered, however, is that the ghost of his father did not urge Hamlet to commit the murder. The plan to kill Claudius was Hamlet's own. His father's ghost had simply told him to "Revenge . . . foul and most

83

unnatural murder." Revenge for murder was traditionally a second murder, but the Ghost is actually very
vague in his suggestions to Hamlet: ". . . howsoever
thou pursuest this act . . ." The point is that Hamlet
is not given a sacred command by his dead father to
kill. That command is imposed by himself upon himself. In his failure to act, Hamlet does not betray a
promise to any outside person. Rather he proves himself unable to honor a self-imposed decision to commit
murder.

The problem of *Hamlet* may be looked at in one of
two ways. The first would be to say that the decision
to plan and commit a murder, for whatever reason, is
too terrible and too evil a decision for any sane and
intelligent man to carry out at any time. And the
second would be to say that murder is a possible action
for a rational man to plan and to commit, but Hamlet
was unable to perform the action.

The first theory will probably lead us closer to an
understanding of the play than will the second. For
if Hamlet was unable to do a deed that many men
might have done, then he is again only a special case.
The tragedy would not be holding "a mirror up to
nature," but would be holding a mirror up only to
Hamlet, to one very particular man. It must be remembered, furthermore, that, far from being inactive
or lazy, Hamlet is a man of action. In the course of
the play he pretends to be mad; he insults Ophelia; he
argues with his mother; in a moment of passion and
self-defense, he kills Polonius; he escapes from imprisonment; he fights a duel. He is able to do many

things. What he cannot do is deliberately and soberly plot a murder, and then commit it.

Why is Hamlet unable to do this? The answer to the question is perhaps the most simple and obvious answer that could be furnished: because he did not want to.

Shakespeare was writing before the day of applied psychology with its theories of conscious and unconscious motivation, but he was, as a poet, fully aware of many of the reasons for human behavior. Hamlet says that he wants to murder Claudius. He does not murder him. He is sane and healthy. It must be concluded that he does not murder Claudius because he does not really want to, despite what he says. He knows very well that "an eye for an eye, a tooth for a tooth" is an immoral and useless system of justice. He unconsciously knows that no good can be accomplished through revenge. Hamlet is tugged at on one side by the way of the world, and on the other by the way of Heaven. He asks himself, "What should such fellows as I do, crawling between heaven and earth?" Put another way, it is the animal in man that makes Hamlet kill Polonius and Rosencrantz and Guildenstern for reasons of unthinking self-defense. The spiritual part of man prevents him from plotting and carrying out a murder that is not concerned with his own physical and personal safety.

Hamlet is a drama of the spiritual side of man in conflict with the animal side. Hamlet, like many men, would rather listen to the spiritual side of his nature: "Judge not. Be merciful. Forgive. Do not kill." But like many men, too, he voices the urgings of his animal side: "Revenge. Defend yourself. Suffer no insults. Kill, if necessary." It is the warring of Hamlet's two sides that is the story of the tragedy. And the tragedy can be applied to everyone, because all men, like Hamlet, are made up of both the spiritual and the physical. Or, to quote the words of William Hazlitt on the tragedy: "It is we who are Hamlet."

The tale of the tragedy of Hamlet was not original with Shakespeare. He turned to two kinds of sources to write the play: literary and historical. Among the literary sources was a history of Denmark written in the twelfth century by a man named Saxo Grammaticus. His *Historia Danica* was translated into French in 1576, and Shakespeare may have read this version, or may have heard of some of the events in it. The story of Hamlet had already been dramatized once, about the year 1590, perhaps by Thomas Kyd, a poet who was a friend of Christopher Marlowe's. That play— *Ur-Hamlet*, as it is referred to today—has been lost, but Shakespeare undoubtedly knew it.

The historical sources of Shakespeare's *Hamlet* are more difficult to trace. The events surrounding the death of the father of King James VI of Scotland (later James I of England) resemble some of the events surrounding the death of Hamlet's father. James' father was murdered, perhaps with his mother's connivance, and almost certainly by the man who later married his mother. There is also reason to suppose that Lord Burghley, Queen Elizabeth's Lord Treasurer and, virtually, prime minister, was caricatured by Shakespeare as Polonius in *Hamlet*. Many readers, too, have noticed that Hamlet and Horatio bear a resemblance to the Earl of Essex and the Earl of Southampton. Inevitably, Shakespeare had Essex and Southampton in his mind to a certain extent while he was writing *Hamlet;* the two noblemen were very much in the public eye while Shakespeare was writing the tragedy. Shakespeare undoubtedly took hints from history and current events, and ideas from his reading, when he wrote *Hamlet,* as he did when he wrote all of his plays. But the greatness of Shakespeare's works depends not on his sources nor on the partial models that he took for his characters. It depends on his conscious and unconscious understanding of the hearts and minds of people; in other words, on his genius.

Hamlet was a popular play. Within ten years, three printed editions of it had been put on sale. The editions, known technically as the First Quarto, the Second Quarto, and the Third Quarto (a quarto is a book in which each sheet of paper, before binding and cutting, has been folded twice so as to form four leaves, or eight pages), may or may not be faithful transcriptions of the text as Shakespeare wrote it; but their mere existence proves that there was great demand for the play immediately after it had been written. It is not difficult to understand why the play was well received. There was, after all, something in it for everyone. There is the famous duel at the end; there is the ghost; the play within the play; wit; humor; pathos; and philosophy. Above all, there is the figure of Hamlet himself, the melancholy Dane, thirty years old, dressed in black, thinking, talking, planning, speak-

ing some of the wittiest and some of the most beautiful and most profound words that have ever been pro-
nounced.

Good night, sweet prince,
And flights of angels sing thee to thy rest!

The popularity of *Hamlet* proved to have material
advantages. Artists—poets, painters, and musicians
—are often thought of as starving geniuses, living in
misery, and producing noble works that go unnoticed
by an insensitive and nonpaying public. Whatever the
fate of other artists, Shakespeare was not a starving
genius. He was paid for his work, and paid well; and
he did not waste the money that he earned. He invested
it in property. In 1597, he had bought New Place in
Stratford. On May 1, 1602, he spent the sum of £320
(about $30,000 today) for 127 acres of land five miles
north of Stratford. In 1605, he invested £440 (about
$40,000) in more Stratford property. A man who has
$70,000 to invest over the space of three years is a rich
man, whether he is living in Elizabethan England or
in twentieth-century New York. Shakespeare owned
shares in the Chamberlain's Men. He was paid for his
acting and he earned money from his writings. William Shakespeare had gone to London to make his
fortune, and he certainly did just that.

In 1603, Queen Elizabeth of England was sixty-nine
years old, and her health was failing. She suffered
from insomnia, an infected throat, and constant thirst.

Yet she would not stay in bed. She walked incessantly up and down her room, and when she was too tired to walk, she sat on cushions on the floor.

Finally, one day she was too sick to get up, but she refused to allow herself to be carried to her bed. She sat on the floor for four days and four nights, saying nothing, eating nothing, and sleeping very little. At last, on the fifth day, she was too faint to protest at being put to bed. She was now far too ill to carry on any state business but she indicated that she wished her successor (she had no natural heirs) to be King James VI of Scotland. On the night of March 23, she became unconscious. It is said that, mysteriously, on that night the whole city of London was wrapped in complete silence. At a quarter to three in the morning, March 24, 1603, Queen Elizabeth I died.

7. The Tragedies of King James' Reign

The new monarch had been James VI of Scotland; now he was James I of England. Two weeks after Elizabeth died, he crossed the River Tweed and began his progress south toward London. He spent two months on the journey, feasting, drinking, hunting, and generously raising to knighthood about five gentlemen a day. James had lived all his life in a politically troubled Scotland. He now fully intended to enjoy his reign as king of a prosperous and powerful England.

James was thirty-seven years old. He was an intelligent and well-educated man. He had written and published several books, and he was to publish more as king of England, including *A Counterblast to Tobacco*, in which he argued that smoking was a dirty and dangerous habit. He was a short man, and rather fat; and he looked fatter than he was because he wore several extra layers of underclothing as protection against a would-be assassin's dagger. James lived in constant fear of assassination, and well he might: both of his parents had died violent deaths. His legs were weak, and therefore he spent as much time as possible on horseback. His eyes looked dull, and he had a habit of letting his mouth hang open. But for all that he was generous, quick-witted, and sincerely desirous of being a good king—as well as a merry one. His wife, Princess Anne of Denmark, was a plain-looking, sharp-tongued, intelligent woman, who, like her husband, had a large appetite for entertainment. She was twenty-eight years old in 1603, and had three children that had survived infancy—Prince Henry, Princess Elizabeth, and Prince Charles, who was to become the ill-fated Charles I of England. (He was sentenced to death and beheaded in 1649 on charges of treason.)

Since both King James and his wife were so fond of entertainment, it was obvious that the actors' companies could look forward to entering on prosperous times. The Chamberlain's Men were singled out for particular honors. On May 19, one week after he had arrived in London, James declared that he would be the patron of the Chamberlain's Men, who were therefore to be known from then on as the King's Men. They were to be paid £10 for every performance at Court. Elizabeth had authorized only about six or seven court performances each year, but James wanted at least twenty. For this new dignity and financial benefit, Shakespeare must have felt grateful to the king. He had another reason for being grateful, as well. James pardoned the Earl of Southampton for his part in the Essex Rebellion, and released him from prison.

In spite of the new king's generosity and good intentions, his reign did not begin happily. No sooner had he reached London, than the plague descended upon the city. The epidemic of 1603 was to be the worst that England had known for many years. Over thirty thousand people died before the disease had worn itself out. For one whole year London was in the grip of fear and death. Every person that could leave the city, did so. All stray animals were rounded up and killed—though had the authorities understood the disease a little better, they would have spared at least the dogs, since dogs would have helped to kill the rats that carried the plague. Householders painted their windows and doors with perfumes and creams of various kinds. Those houses in which plague victims lived were sealed up by the authorities, and no one was allowed to enter or leave. It was hoped that the infection could be blocked in this way. In spite of all these measures—and indeed because of some of them—the plague raged on. James I was crowned in a nearly empty Westminster Abbey. All public gatherings of any kind had been forbidden.

The theaters remained closed because of the plague until April, 1604. Shakespeare probably spent much of the preceding year, and several months of 1604, in Stratford. He was at work on two plays, *Othello* and *Measure for Measure*.

Like *The Merchant of Venice*, *Measure for Measure* is technically a comedy, since none of the principal

characters die, and at the end plans are made for feast-
ings and marriages. It is, however, one of the most
dark and bitter pieces that Shakespeare ever wrote.

Angelo, the central figure, decides to carry out a
moral reform in the city of Vienna, but he is himself
a cruel, dishonest, and hypocritical person. Isabella,
beneath a sincere desire to be high-minded and moral,
is unconsciously cold and pitiless, unwilling to com-
promise her principles even to save her brother's life.
Angelo and Isabella act out their stark and heartless
drama against a background of puns, jokes, and im-
proprieties that serve chiefly to emphasize the bitter
examples that Shakespeare gives of "man's inhuman-
ity to man." *Measure for Measure* has never been one
of Shakespeare's more popular works. Some readers
have found its humor a little indecent. Others feel that
Shakespeare may have been attacking conventional
morality in this play. Some argue that Angelo is too
wicked a man to have been allowed to go free at the
end. (And Angelo is probably the most thoroughly
vicious and evil man that Shakespeare ever created.)
Whatever the justice of these accusations may be,
it cannot be denied that *Measure for Measure* is an
extremely subtle and complex work. It is not a pretty
play, and it is not a pleasant one. It does, however,
unflinchingly hold a mirror up to nature. Perhaps
people see parts of their own lives reflected in it, and
perhaps this is the reason that the play has never
been very popular.

Othello, on the other hand, is one of Shakespeare's best-known and best-liked plays. Indeed, of
his five great tragedies—*Hamlet, Othello, King Lear,*

Macbeth, and *Antony and Cleopatra—Othello* is, with *Hamlet*, the play most often presented, and the one most frequently referred to in conversation. Part of the reason lies in the apparent simplicity of the play, in the sense that the cast is small and the action takes place in only two places, the city of Venice and the island of Cyprus. There is no subplot; there are few excursions into humor or music. *Othello* is also the Shakespearian tragedy that is closest to what may be called normal, daily human life.

Othello is the general of the armies of the Republic of Venice. He is a middle-aged Negro, tall, handsome, strong, brave, tender, and generous. He falls in love with Desdemona, a Venetian girl, and they elope. Othello is sent by the Venetian government on a military expedition to Cyprus, and Desdemona goes with him. In Cyprus, Iago, an ensign in Othello's service, hints to his general that Desdemona is not a faithful wife. He implies and suggests so cleverly and so vigorously that Othello is finally convinced of his wife's dishonesty. He accuses Desdemona to her face. She replies that she has been entirely faithful, as indeed she has been; but Othello refuses to believe her. He murders her, and, when five minutes afterward he learns that Iago has lied, he kills himself.

Readers and spectators of this tragedy inevitably ask themselves two questions: Why did Iago lie so viciously? and why did Othello believe what Iago told him?

Many people have argued that Iago had no reason at all for acting as he did. They say that he is a wholly evil creature who does evil for its own sake. Others point out that Iago was angry because Othello had not given him the promotion that he thought that he had deserved. It is often said that Othello is, indeed, brave, generous, and tender, but that he is also jealous by nature. His jealousy emerges, of course, only after he has fallen in love and married. Fanned to white heat by Iago, that jealousy causes him to murder, entirely unreasonably, the only person that he has ever really loved, or that has, perhaps, loved him.

These answers contain a portion of truth, but they are perhaps not complete or entirely satisfactory as they stand. Iago is certainly an evil man in the fullest sense. He is also angry at not having been promoted. Othello does become violently and almost insanely jealous. Yet these three factors alone do not seem to explain why Desdemona was murdered.

A careful look at the play shows that it was not Iago's original intention, when he started his campaign of slander, to go so far as to bring about the murder of Desdemona. He was angry because Othello had not promoted him, and he decided, therefore, to pay Othello back by needling him and upsetting him. His plan was to take away Othello's peace of mind, and to destroy the bliss of his honeymoon. Although it was an evil plan, it was not a plot to have Desdemona murdered. Othello, however, reacted unexpectedly. On the one hand, he believed Iago more quickly and more implicitly than could have been expected and he swore to murder Desdemona if she really had been unfaithful. On the other hand, he threatened to kill Iago, if

Iago did not furnish absolute proof that what he hinted was true. Thus Iago found himself in a situation in which either he must lose his life or Desdemona must lose hers. If he had possessed any decency at all, he would, of course, at this point, have written Othello a note confessing everything and have vanished forever from the scene. But he did not do this. Rather, he strengthened and extended his lies. He furnished what Othello took to be absolute proof, and Desdemona was killed. Ironically, Iago does not die in the play. He, the malefactor, survives.

But why did Othello, a generous and loving man, believe so implicitly the vicious lies that were told him about his own wife? There are many reasons. They may not account completely for the great error that Othello committed, but some of them, at least, are worth looking at. In the first place, it was Desdemona's father and not Iago that first planted the seed of jealousy in Othello's mind. Enraged because his daughter has eloped, he says to Othello:

> Look to her, Moor, if thou hast eyes to see:
> She has deceived her father and may, thee.

In the second place, Othello is twenty or twenty-five years older than Desdemona, and he is a military man, used to the camp and the battlefield, and not to the parlor and to married life. He fears that Desdemona might be bored with his blunt and unsophisticated company. Othello is confident of his abilities as a soldier, but he is unsure of himself as a husband. In the third place, Iago's campaign is very shrewd. Although evil and immoral, Iago is clever and astute. The arguments that he uses and the proofs that he furnishes in order to convince Othello of Desdemona's unfaithfulness are, for the most part, very ingenious.

Yet Shakespeare certainly did not create a villain such as Iago, a man "great of heart" such as Othello, and a beautiful Venetian girl such as Desdemona, in order simply to depict scenes of domestic strife. There are deeper emotions at work than simply suspicion and jealousy. Indeed, it is not too much to say that one of the most heartbreaking and terrifying moments of all dramatic literature occurs in *Othello*, in Act IV. Othello, in a blind rage for his belief that Desdemona has betrayed him, and before guests that have come to visit him, cries out to her, "Devil!" and strikes her full in the face. Desdemona, who adores her husband and cannot imagine why he should be so brutal, hangs her head and says simply, "I have not deserved this." The horror that the audience and the reader feel at this moment is sure proof that a situation exists that must have its roots in something deeper than a mere family quarrel.

Love, it is said, often causes pain. Literature, from poetry to popular songs, tells us as much. Although we do not know for certain why Othello killed Desdemona, it is surely true that he killed her because he loved her, and not because his jealousy made him hate her. Naturally, every man does not kill the woman he loves, and few murders are actually committed for reasons of true love. Even so, the reader feels that

Othello truly loved Desdemona, and that she truly loved him. And he killed her.

The search for why Othello murdered his wife leads to one final and strange fact about the play. Othello, Desdemona, and Iago all arrive in Cyprus late one Saturday afternoon. By about 11:30 the next night —thirty-one hours later—Othello has murdered Desdemona. In other words, it took Iago only a little more than one day to convince Othello that Desdemona was an unfaithful wife. Obviously, between Saturday afternoon and Sunday evening, with her husband always near her, Desdemona did not have the time to be unfaithful in any sense. Yet Othello is convinced of her dishonesty.

Was Othello simply an incredible fool to think something possible that was obviously impossible? If that were true, there would be no tragedy, for Othello would become a special case, an example of utter imbecility. Did Shakespeare make a mistake by calculating the time wrong? Shakespeare did make several technical mistakes in many of his plays, but he did not ever commit a blunder of this size. He certainly did not go so far as to invalidate a whole drama by making a careless error in time sequences.

A closer look at *Othello* shows that its characters are "huge cloudy symbols of a high romance." Othello is the Moorish general but he is also all men who love directly and truly and simply; and Desdemona is a young Venetian girl and at the same time she is all women loving and beloved. Ideally, love is a drawing together, the union of two hearts and minds and bodies.

98

But the growth of love toward complete union takes time, and love, by temperament, is impatient.

Othello cannot wait. Iago speeds up his actions and reactions. Affection which is "speeded up" becomes possessiveness; tenderness becomes brutality. Love that will not wait becomes cruelty and violence, and can even become murder. Othello kills Desdemona because he loves her and will not wait. Entirely unconscious of the fact that he is doing so, he seeks the immediate total fusion of himself with her. His physical body and hers prevent that fusion. He must kill her to free her spirit from her body, if his spirit is to mingle with hers. (Brutus expresses, though under very different circumstances, a not too different process of thought: "O! then that we could come by Caesar's spirit, and not dismember Caesar. But, alas! Caesar must bleed for it.") If Othello had been more patient and more wise, he would have waited. If his conscious thoughts had dominated his unconscious mind, he would have let his love be realized in the birth of life, rather than in death. But he was neither patient nor wise; his conscious thoughts did not guide his actions. Just before he committed suicide, he recognized his horrendous error, and truly described himself as "one that loved not wisely, but too well."

Although the London theaters remained closed during 1603 because of the plague, a few plays were performed at court for King James and his family. One of these was a tragedy named *Sejanus*, written by Ben Jonson. The cast of characters for one production of *Sejanus* contains the name of Shakespeare; and it is the last record that we have of Shakespeare as an actor. He may have appeared in a few performances after 1603, but probably in not many. Until this time, he had been thought of by his friends and colleagues as an actor who also wrote plays. Now he was regarded as a playwright who also, on occasion, was an actor.

It is not surprising that Shakespeare retired as an actor. In 1603, he was nearly forty years old, and acting, in his time, was far more strenuous work than it is today. An actor in the seventeenth century was expected to be also a singer, a dancer, and something of an acrobat. He had to have a loud and powerful voice. It was necessary for him to know at least one part in about twenty plays, and to be ready to act in any one of those at sometimes no more than a day's notice. Shakespeare perhaps now preferred to save all his energy for his writing.

Ben Jonson, the author of many plays besides *Sejanus*, was eight years younger than Shakespeare, and was just beginning to make a name for himself about 1600. He was a big, warmhearted, but quarrelsome man, who had narrowly escaped hanging for having killed a fellow actor in a duel. He was also a good scholar, and at times a great poet. Although a conceited man and over-certain of his own abilities, he was able to recognize genius when he saw it. He saw it in his friend Shakespeare. On one occasion he condensed into just ten words his opinion of Shakespeare's literary genius, and it is doubtful that a clearer or truer estimate of Shakespeare has ever been given. Jonson said, "He was not for an age, but for all time."

While Shakespeare was in London between 1600 and 1605, he boarded with a family named Mountjoy. The Mountjoys lived a few blocks north of St. Paul's Cathedral, not far from the Fortune theater. Christopher Mountjoy was an attire-maker. An attire was a costly headdress worn by fashionable ladies of the time. It was a large net of gold thread into which pearls, rubies, and emeralds were sewn. Attire-making was a difficult and respected craft, and a good attire-maker was a man almost as much in the news at that time as a first-class fashion designer is today. Christopher Mountjoy was one of the leading men in the field, and had made attires for Queen Elizabeth. Obviously, he was a man who did not rent a room to Shakespeare simply because he needed a little extra money. It is not known when Shakespeare and Mountjoy first became friends, or why Shakespeare stayed with the family in London. But the fact that he did stay with them proves that he had neither bought nor rented a house for himself in the city. This, in turn, would tend to show that after 1600, Shakespeare did not spend many weeks at a time away from Stratford.

Just behind St. Paul's Cathedral, on Bread Street, about five minutes' walk from the Mountjoys' house, was the Mermaid Tavern. It was there that Shakespeare and Ben Jonson probably got to know each other, since the Mermaid was the gathering-place for many of the writers and artists of the day. Among its patrons were Inigo Jones, the famous architect who designed the sets for productions at court; John Donne, the poet, who in 1621 was named dean of St. Paul's Cathedral; and two young men named Francis Beaumont and John Fletcher, later to collaborate in writing plays. And there were also Shakespeare and Ben Jonson.

These various men usually met on Friday evenings at the Mermaid, and the first Friday of every month was their big meeting. They ate a good meal together. (There is a record of a fine that the manager of the Mermaid, William Johnson, was forced to pay for having served meat to "the worshipful fraternity" on several of those occasions. Friday was by law a fish-eating day in Elizabethan England.) Some of the men probably "took a pipe of tobacco"; smoking a pipe was a fashionable new habit at the time. And they talked. There are two chief references to the conversations at the Mermaid. One was written several years later by Francis Beaumont:

What things have we seen
Done at the Mermaid! heard words that have been,
So nimble, and so full of subtle flame,
As if that every one from whence they came
Had meant to put his whole wit in a jest,
And had resolved to live a fool the rest
Of his dull life.

The other was also written several years later by a historian named Thomas Fuller:

William Shakespeare . . . was an eminent instance of the truth of that rule, *poeta non fit, sed nascitur,* one is not *made*, but *born* a poet. Indeed, his learning was very little. . . .

Many were the *wit-combats* betwixt him and Ben Jonson, which two I behold like a *Spanish great galleon* and an *English Man of War*; Master Jonson . . . was built far higher in learning; solid but slow in his performances. *Shake-speare*, with the English Man of War, lesser in bulk, but lighter in sailing, could turn with all tides, tack about and take advantage of all winds, by the quickness of his wit and invention.

Although Fuller does not mention the Mermaid Tavern by name, it is fairly certain that the "wit-combats" that he mentions took place there. In any case, his words are some of the most interesting that we have about Shakespeare: ". . . one is not made, but born a poet. . . . Shakespeare . . . could turn with all tides. . . ."

Now a picture of Shakespeare begins to emerge. In our imagination, we see him as not a tall man or a fat man. He was neatly dressed. He was soft-spoken and just a little shy. He listened more than he talked, watching the expressions on his companions' faces. He sympathized with Beaumont's ambitions, and with Donne's complicated sense of sorrow and bafflement. He enjoyed Jonson's loud, forceful, energetic pronouncements. As the evening wore on, he entered more into the conversation. His sentences were short; his words, well-chosen; his voice, calm and quiet. The other men listened to him, feeling perhaps that he was somehow a little different from them. He did not talk of voyages, adventures, business speculations, or crimes and politics. He liked these topics but he was more interested in what people thought and felt, in why they did what they did. His conversation was directed toward a man's sense of right and wrong, toward sorrow and love, toward life and death, heaven and hell. The other men would listen, and then return to the telling of anecdotes and stories, and Shakespeare in his turn would listen, and remember. If a story interested him particularly, he would ask to have it told in detail, or he would make a mental note to read it himself later. Finally, he would rise quietly and walk home through the dark streets to the Mountjoys' house, and spend several hours writing or reading by the light of a candle.

One evening at the Mermaid the conversation turned to Scottish history. Since the new king was a Scotsman, surely it would be a good idea, someone said, to write a play based on Scottish history. King James would like that. Several eyes turned to Shakespeare. He had already written a play set in Denmark. Had he done so, he was asked, because James' wife was Danish? Was that why his thoughts had turned to the story of Hamlet? Did he not agree, in any case, that a play set in Scotland would be a good idea? Shakespeare may have proposed that Jonson do the play: after all, Jonson was partly Scottish on his father's side. But if Jonson was asked, he must have refused because, in the end, it was Shakespeare that wrote the "Scottish play." It is the tragedy of *Macbeth*.

Of the five great Shakespearian tragedies, *Hamlet*

and *Othello* have much in common, as do *Macbeth* and *King Lear*. *Antony and Cleopatra* stands by itself. *Hamlet* and *Othello* are tragedies that are assaults upon the mind. *Macbeth* and *King Lear* assault the heart. The tragedies of Hamlet and Othello grow out of their minds, out of a momentary breakdown of their abilities to think rightly, or with the utmost clarity and vigor. As we read their tragic stories, we feel sorrow and desperation for their destinies because we are puzzled by the minds of these two men which lead them to pain and death, rather than to happiness and life. This is not so with either *Macbeth* or *King Lear*. Our reaction to both these plays is an emotional one more than it is a mental one.

Macbeth and *King Lear* were probably written by Shakespeare one right after the other, during the years 1605 and 1606. We do not know which was written first.

Macbeth is one of Shakespeare's shortest plays, containing just 2,108 lines. It is a vigorous, headlong drama, a relentless spectacle in red and black. Macbeth and Banquo, two Scottish generals, are stopped by three witches on a heath, who predict that Macbeth will become king of Scotland and that Banquo's descendants will become the Scottish royal family. Macbeth tells his wife of this meeting, and when King Duncan is staying at their castle, together (in a sense) they murder him. Duncan's sons, Malcolm and Donalbain, are suspected of the crime and they flee. Macbeth is crowned king. In order to defeat the witches' prediction concerning Banquo, Macbeth

105

plots the murder of both Banquo and his son. Although Banquo is killed, his son escapes. The Scottish nobles now begin to suspect how Duncan really met his death, and Macbeth resorts to more murders in the hope of keeping his throne. Finally, an army is sent against him. Lady Macbeth goes mad and dies. Macbeth is killed in hand-to-hand combat by Macduff, and peace returns to Scotland.

In one way, *Macbeth* is the most remarkable of all of Shakespeare's plays. After Macbeth and his wife are dead, they are described by Malcolm as "this dead butcher and his fiend-like queen." The description is absolutely correct. Yet in spite of its truth, in spite of the fact that the audience detests what Macbeth and his wife have done, neither character completely loses the viewer's sympathy. We do not ever hope that they will be allowed to go free to commit more mayhem and murder. We cannot imagine that they will ever repent and begin to lead decent lives. We cannot, however, hate them.

Shakespeare did not at any time, in any of his plays —and this point cannot be emphasized too strongly— try to preach, teach, advocate, persuade, or judge. He might have said of himself, with another English poet, William Blake, "I am hid." After having read all of Shakespeare's plays, no reader can ever be absolutely sure of what Shakespeare himself thought on any subject. All that is known is what his characters thought. *Macbeth*, and *King Lear*, are Shakespeare's most black and pessimistic works, and Macbeth is one of the most bitter of all the characters in the history of literature. The speech that he delivers when the news is brought to him that his wife has died is one of Shakespeare's most famous pieces of writing. It is also one of the blackest pictures of human existence that has ever been painted (V, v).

Macbeth.   Wherefore was that cry?
Seyton.   The queen, my lord, is dead.
Macbeth. She should have died hereafter;
   There would have been a time for such a word.
   To-morrow, and to-morrow, and to-morrow,
   Creeps in this petty pace from day to day,
   To the last syllable of recorded time;
   And all our yesterdays have lighted fools
   The way to dusty death. Out, out, brief candle!
   Life's but a walking shadow, a poor player
   That struts and frets his hour upon the stage
   And then is heard no more; it is a tale
   Told by an idiot, full of sound and fury,
   Signifying nothing.

". . . Signifying nothing": it must only be remembered that it was Macbeth, and not William Shakespeare, that thought this and said this about life. And who was Macbeth? What sort of man was he?

Macbeth was a man who discovered, to his complete undoing, that the getting and holding of political power can too easily destroy a man's capacity for using that power well. Indeed, we might legitimately strike the word "political" out of the consideration: Macbeth's drama and tragedy is the drama and tragedy of all men who want power and position for their own sake and at any price. *Macbeth* is the tragedy of the swelling of the ego and of the growth of vainglory.

In the third act, after Macbeth has murdered Banquo, the Ghost of Banquo returns to haunt him. Macbeth has now lost all ability to distinguish right from wrong. He has passed, as it were, beyond good and evil. And yet, he remains completely sane:

> I am in blood
> Stepp'd in so far that, should I wade no more,
> Returning were as tedious as go o'er.

After this moment of pure sorrow and pure evil, Macbeth is living his human life in hell.

But Macbeth was not always corrupt. When the play opens, he is a brave and noble Scottish soldier. The story of Macbeth is the story of a man's fall from grace and excellence to the bottom of the abyss of evil. He falls so swiftly that our minds become too dizzy to follow his descent. It is impossible for us to pause and to say, "This is the cause, this is where Macbeth began to go wrong." We can only watch his total disintegration, and become breathless with anguish as we watch.

From the moment that the witches speak in Act I, both Macbeth and Lady Macbeth, who are equal in their viciousness, know only one moment of grace. That moment comes at different times for each of them. For Macbeth, it is the minute just after the murder of King Duncan. He is frightened and horrified by what he has done. He is even for an instant truly repentant. A knock is heard at the door.

Wake Duncan with thy knocking! I would thou couldst!

But he forgets his penitence and he goes on to become stronger, more powerful, more evil and violent. For the armies sent to seize him, he has nothing but brave contempt:

We might have met them dareful, beard to beard,
And beat them backward home.

When he sees that he is surrounded, that he must be killed, and even knowing that he deserves to be killed, he will not yield:

Why should I play the Roman fool, and die
On mine own sword?

Here is no pensive, philosophical Brutus, no grief-stricken Othello. Macbeth's final words are a supreme, ferocious challenge to destiny:

Yet will I try the last: before my body
I throw my war-like shield. Lay on, Macduff,
And damned be him that first cries "Hold,
    enough!"

Lady Macbeth's moment of repentance comes just before her death. Mercifully, she goes nearly mad; and in her near-madness is able to understand what she could not understand before. She sees the brutality and the cruelty of what she has done. She relives, sleepwalking, the time when she and her husband murdered Duncan. She rubs her hands together constantly, believing that she is trying to wash off the blood with which they are stained. She remembers the way in which she encouraged her husband to kill the king, and she pronounces to herself now similar phrases of encouragement, bitterly half-aware of the hollowness of their meaning:

Fie, my lord, fie! A soldier, and afeard?

Suddenly, she sees the exact moment of the murder, and she now says what some part of her had then thought, but did not say:

Yet who would have thought the old man to have had so much blood in him?

Finally, in her imagination, she turns to Macbeth:

Come, give me your hand. What's done cannot be undone.

It has been said that perhaps the reason that the reader never altogether loses sympathy—even affection—for Macbeth and Lady Macbeth is that they are, at least on the surface of things, a most happily married couple. Although "happily married" seem strange words to use about two such terrifying people, they do apply. Macbeth and his wife talk freely and openly with each other. They encourage and help each other. They are each ambitious for the other's welfare. In a word, they love each other. It is true that in killing the king they destroyed themselves. It is also true that

110

in the course of the play, they drift apart, as Macbeth increases in vigor and power, while Lady Macbeth withdraws into the shadows. But even when they have drifted apart, neither blames the other for their hideous situation. And Lady Macbeth's last words are pathetic attempts to console her husband. Not one word of reproof ever escapes the lips of either of them.

This is the drama that Shakespeare wrote, based on Scottish history, to please a Scottish-born king. He had found the story of Macbeth in *The Chronicles of England, Scotland and Ireland*, by Raphael Holinshed, published in 1577. *The Chronicles* also contained the outlines of a story that Shakespeare would turn into his fourth great tragedy, an even more bitter and terrible tragedy than *Macbeth*—*King Lear*.

King Lear was monarch of Britain more than a thousand years before the birth of Christ. As Shakespeare tells the story, Lear is an old man of eighty. He has decided to give up his throne, to divide his kingdom into three parts, and to turn them over to his three daughters. He also decides to hold a brief ceremony, at the moment in which he is actually going to give his kingdom away. During this ceremony, he asks each of his daughters to tell him how much she loves him. Goneril and Regan, the two oldest, make flowery speeches in which they tell their father of the greatness of the love that they feel for him. Cordelia, the third daughter, is repelled by her two sisters' speeches. She knows that they do not mean what they are saying. Therefore, she makes a short speech, saying very

111

simply that she loves her father, but she adds no flowery phrases to say how much. Lear becomes violently angry at what he thinks is Cordelia's coldheartedness. He does not understand that Cordelia really loves him, and that Goneril and Regan do not. He takes Cordelia's share of the kingdom and divides it between her two sisters. He also banishes his good friend and wise counselor, the Earl of Kent, who has tried to defend Cordelia. The youngest daughter accepts a proposal of marriage from the king of France, and leaves Britain. Goneril and Regan shortly afterward refuse to have their father in their houses. Lear, accompanied by the Fool, must wander out and spend the night of a terrible thunderstorm on an open heath. There he meets Edgar, the son of the Earl of Gloucester, who has been unjustly banished by his father. During the storm, Lear goes mad. When he regains his sanity, he finds that Cordelia has returned to Britain with an army led by her husband, to protect her father from Goneril and Regan, and from Edmund, Edgar's evil brother. Edmund orders Cordelia to be murdered. The French army is defeated. Goneril, in a fit of jealousy, murders Regan, and then commits suicide. When Lear discovers that Cordelia is dead, he dies of a broken heart.

On the surface, this story has something of the fairy tale about it. There are two bad sisters, and one good sister, and there is a handsome king to marry the good sister. There is a terrible thunderstorm in which terrible things happen. The very opening of the play, too, has the air of a fairy tale about it. Lear's plan to have his daughters each recite a little love speech is both a sweet and a foolish idea. What harm could possibly come of it? Yet *King Lear*, in the opinion of many people, is the saddest of Shakespeare's tragedies.

As a drama, it is certainly the most complex. *King Lear* has two distinct plots which Shakespeare gradually weaves into one. There are eleven major characters that we must carefully follow. The whole action of the play occurs at a time which is remote from us. The atmosphere that Shakespeare's language creates is dark and gray. Both the people and the places in *King Lear* appear as vague and shadowy forms.

King Lear is both so complex and so shadowy that it is not easy even to say exactly what the play is about. As we read it, we are deeply and bitterly moved; but it is not easy to say why we are.

Perhaps the first thing to keep in mind when reading *King Lear* is that Lear himself is a very old man. It is not often that plays or books are written about very old people. As a result, we are apt to think of Lear as a man of fifty or so. But he is not fifty. He is over eighty. He has passed the limits of the biblical life span by more than ten years. Inevitably, he has all the weaknesses and failings of very old age. He is changeable and querulous, stubborn, set in his ways, and very sentimental. When Lear briefly goes mad, we are not witnessing an unexpected excursion into insanity by a vigorous mind. His madness is another aspect of his great age.

Lear has been king of Britain for many years. We should expect him to be proud and stately and digni-

113

fied. He is none of these. Traditionally, age brings wisdom. We should expect Lear's thoughts to be poised and balanced and profound. They are not. Lear, however, once describes himself thoroughly and accurately. After his period of madness, and when Cordelia has returned to Britain, in his regained sanity, he says this of himself (IV, vii):

> I am a very foolish fond old man,
> Fourscore and upward . . .
> And, to deal plainly,
> I fear I am not in my perfect mind . . .
>   . . . Do not laugh at me;
> For, as I am a man . . .

(In Elizabethan English, "fond" did not mean "affectionate," but "simple" or "silly.") *As I am a man* is perhaps the phrase that we ought to remember more than any other as we read *King Lear*.

Lear is a great and powerful monarch. He gives his kingdom away. Immediately his trappings, his prestige, his authority, and his splendor vanish, too. Having given away his kingdom, Lear is no longer a king but simply and only another man. Lear has three daughters. Two of them abandon him, and he abandons the third. Suddenly, he has no family, no home, no physical comforts, no domestic affections. Lear is no longer a loving and beloved father. He is simply a lonely, solitary man. Lear is very old. He should have been wise, but his reason deserts him. He cannot, for a time, fully understand what is said to him, nor can he express himself coherently. He becomes a man in isolation, imprisoned within the walls of his own defective mind. Yet what he says during the time when his "wits have turned" is perhaps wiser and truer than many of the things that he said at the beginning of the play when his mind was sound.

Shakespeare created a great person and then took from him everything that might set him above, or apart from, his fellow beings. He even took away his reason, man's most cherished faculty. Without his worldly trappings, Lear is not a king. Without his daughters, he is not a father. Is he, without his reason, no longer even a man? During the thunderstorm on the heath, Lear tries to tear off his clothes. Is a man without reason, family, or possessions merely a naked animal? *King Lear* is a play about that question—one of the oldest that has ever been asked: What is man?

No direct and simple answer is given, naturally enough, even in the complex fabric of *King Lear*. We do, however, see one thing clearly in the course of the play. When a man is deprived of everything, including his reason, and yet is still alive, he has one remaining possession, one attribute: affection, the capacity to love and to be loved. Even in his wretchedness and misery, Lear is not entirely alone. He is accompanied by the Fool, who loves Lear, and will not desert him.

The Fool has no "reason" to love Lear, and if he had, we would not expect a fool to understand it or to act on it. Any fool, and this one in particular, has no education and no learning. He really has no normally functioning mind. He does not hope to get anything from Lear: neither money nor privileges and power.

115

His affection for Lear is entirely disinterested. But he has affection. It is perhaps the only thing that he has.

The Fool in *King Lear* (he has no name except "Fool") is one of the most remarkable characters in literature. Among other things, in the midst of this terrible tragedy, he is genuinely funny. Bitter and painful as the play is, we often cannot help laughing when the Fool speaks. At the same time, he is, in fact, the wisest of all of the characters. The Fool is wise because he is loving and loyal and true. We see, in *King Lear*, that true wisdom may lie not in the brain but in the heart. The measure of a man is not what he possesses, not his brilliance nor his intelligence. It is his ability to love and, in loving, to act with honesty, loyalty, and truth. Thus, when at the end of the play, Lear discovers that Cordelia is dead—the person that had loved him most, and that he had loved, though neither had been intelligent enough to show that love, or even to recognize its existence—Lear himself dies of a broken heart.

King Lear is Shakespeare's deepest and most relentless piece of writing. Lear, Act III, says, "Anatomize Regan: see what breeds about her heart." Shakespeare has anatomized the human condition. *King Lear* is a dramatization of something said nearly sixteen hundred years before Shakespeare turned to the writing of tragedy: ". . . though I . . . understand all mysteries, and all knowledge; and though I have all faith . . . and have not love, I am nothing." (In the first act, when Lear asks Cordelia to make her little love speech, he says: "What can you say . . .? Speak." Cordelia's reply is: "Nothing, my lord." "Nothing?" "Nothing.") It might indeed be said that *King Lear* is a religious play set in a world in which there is no religion. The Christian religion and others have always urged man to love his fellowman: "Thou shalt love thy neighbour as thyself." *King Lear* undertakes to show, independently of religious commandments, why we must love our neighbor. It shows that man is man because he is a creature capable of love and affection.

Although sometimes it has been said that Shakespeare must have been in a bitter frame of mind during 1605, 1606, and 1607 to have written such black and desperate tragedies, there is no record of any particularly wretched event in his life at that time. It would seem that, on the contrary, he had every reason to be happy during those years. On June 5, 1607, his daughter Susanna was married to John Hall, a doctor. Hall had studied at Cambridge and also in France. About the year 1600, at the age of twenty-five, he had moved to Stratford. And, he was, perhaps strangely for a man who became the son-in-law of a playwright, a Puritan.

In February, 1608, Shakespeare became a grandfather for the first time. Susanna gave birth to a girl, who was baptized on February 21. She was named Elizabeth.

117

8. Blackfriars Theater

The London theaters, during the reign of James I, continued to stay within the liberties, just as they had during the reign of Elizabeth.

Not far from St. Paul's Cathedral and the Mermaid Tavern was an old Dominican monastery, or priory, known as Blackfriars. It had ceased to function as a religious house in 1538 but it was, for many years after that, a liberty. Some of its buildings had long been in the hands of the Master of the Revels, and from 1576 plays had been presented there by a company of actors known as the Children of the Chapel. These "children" were in many cases actually young men. On several occasions, and in spite of the fact that they were performing within a liberty, the Children of the Chapel had managed to get into trouble because of the plays they performed. Finally, in 1608, because of a play called *The Conspiracy and Tragedy of Byron*, by George Chapman, some of the "children" were sent to prison. One of the characters in the play was the Queen of France, and she gave another character a box on the ear. The French ambassador was enraged at this slur on the French reigning family and he entered a protest. The sheriff had no official power to close the Blackfriars theater. Difficulties, however, could be put in the way of any future performances there—and they were. The Children of the Chapel company was dissolved, and Blackfriars stood empty.

Richard Burbage owned Blackfriars at the time. He decided to reopen it as a winter theater for the King's Men. It would make excellent winter quarters for them because, unlike the Globe, the Curtain, the Swan, and other houses, Blackfriars was a closed building. It much more resembled present-day theaters than did the other London theaters of King James' reign. It was a large hall, somewhat over sixty-five feet long and forty-five feet wide. At the end of the hall was the stage. All of the Blackfriars patrons were to be given a seat, so audiences would, of course, be much smaller than audiences at the Globe, and admission prices would be higher. Performances would be given at night by candlelight. Blackfriars was to be an "intimate theater."

In August, 1608, seven men, six of them members of the King's Men, formed a Blackfriars theater holding company with the intention of developing Blackfriars into a working winter theater. Shakespeare was one of the seven men.

Shakespeare, Burbage, and their five fellow-sharers had undoubtedly intended to open the new theater for the 1608-9 season, but the opening had to be postponed. Once again the plague descended on the city of London. All theaters were closed, and were to stay closed until the end of 1609. The King's Men again spent a year touring the country districts. They were not able to give a performance in their new quarters until the winter of 1609.

While the King's Men were acquiring Blackfriars, Shakespeare was writing his fifth great tragedy, *Antony and Cleopatra*. As he had for *Julius Caesar*, he took his story for this play from North's translation of Plutarch's *Lives*. The play opens in 40 B.C., two years after the battle of Philippi, the point at which *Julius Caesar* had closed. Mark Antony, with Lepidus and Octavius Caesar, is one of the three rulers of the Roman Empire. He is also in love with Cleopatra, queen of Egypt, and he spends a great deal of time at her court in Alexandria. Lepidus and Octavius are not pleased by Antony's behavior. They feel that he is not doing his share of the work of ruling the empire. When Antony's wife dies in Rome, he returns there. He tries to patch up his differences with Octavius by marrying Octavius' sister. Antony leaves her, however, for Cleopatra—and Octavius declares war on him. At the battle of Actium, Antony is defeated because Cleopatra's fighting vessels flee. At a later battle, Antony is surrounded and forced to yield. He believes that in some way Cleopatra has betrayed him again, and has brought about his downfall. Terrified by his wrath, Cleopatra locks herself in her tower and sends word to Antony that she is dead. In grief and despair, Antony commits suicide, but lives long enough to die in Cleopatra's arms. After Antony's death, Cleopatra kills herself.

Antony and Cleopatra is the most colorful spectacle of any of Shakespeare's plays. Its atmosphere is the atmosphere of magnificence that surrounded both the court of the queen of Egypt and the city of Rome in that era. There are battle scenes, banquet scenes, love scenes. There are moments of humor, cruelty, pathos, and grief. And the play contains some of the most exquisite lines of poetry that Shakespeare ever wrote.

The play's tone of power is set by Mark Antony. Whatever history may say about Antony, Shakespeare portrayed him as a great and splendid man. Antony has the vigor that he had in *Julius Caesar* and, as well, the charm and the force of personality of a great and powerful man in the prime of life. He is, to all intents and purposes, the ruler of the civilized world. He is idolized by his followers, respected by his enemies, and adored by Cleopatra:

His face was as the heavens . . .
His legs bestrid the ocean; his rear'd arm
Crested the world . . . in his livery
Walk'd crowns and crownets, realms and islands
   were
As plates dropp'd from his pocket . . .

Shakespeare once again gave to a man everything that the world and that man's own character could give. Once again the man is reduced to grief and anguish, and is driven to self-destruction. Once again the reader is terrified by the man's fall, and must ask "Why?"

Antony's love and passion for Cleopatra is to some degree concerned in his fall. Cleopatra, however, is no ordinary woman. She is worthy of her Antony. She is as great and complex a woman as Antony is a man. No description of her can be more exact than the lines spoken by Enobarbus, Antony's friend and chief lieutenant (Act II):

> Age cannot wither her, nor custom stale
> Her infinite variety.

It is difficult to believe that words of greater praise could ever be written or spoken about any woman.

Antony remains throughout the play a realistic and practical man. His great love for Cleopatra does not blind him to the facts of political life. He knows that unless he abandons her, he will lose his power in the Roman Empire. Yet he does not abandon her. At the opening of the play he says:

> Let Rome in Tiber melt, and the wide arch
> Of the rang'd empire fall! Here is my space . . .

—and by "here" he means "beside Cleopatra." This may sound like mere romantic bravado, but Antony repeats the idea later. After he has lost the battle of Actium, and Cleopatra is weeping—perhaps out of sorrow for her part in Antony's defeat—he says to her:

> Fall not a tear, I say; one of them rates
> All that is won and lost: give me a kiss:
> Even this repays me.

And at the last, after he believes that Cleopatra has contributed to his defeat and, without meaning to, has tricked him into suicide, not a word of reproof escapes his lips:

> I am dying, Egypt, dying; only
> I here importune death awhile, until
> Of many thousand kisses the poor last
> I lay upon thy lips.

Cleopatra was worth the whole world.

We cannot help but wonder how this can be. Can one woman, however fascinating and magnetic, be worth the virtual possession of the whole world? A sentence from the Bible again comes to mind: ''For what is a man profited, if he shall gain the whole world, and lose his own soul?''

In *Antony and Cleopatra*, we see the truth of the role that love between a man and a woman can play in life. When love is true, it is the chief part of man's soul. Although Antony loses the world, the world is temporary. Death will sooner or later cut him off from it. Antony gains Cleopatra, and conserves his love for her, and her love for him. Love, being of the soul, is eternal. Antony has Cleopatra for eternity. He leaves the world—

Unarm, Eros, the long day's task is done
And we must sleep

to gain the eternal world—

    . . . my queen . . . stay for me:
Where souls do couch on flowers, we'll hand in
    hand . . .

Antony—not unlike Hamlet—does not follow what seem to be the traditional rules of human society. Instead of being willing to do anything to keep the riches and the power that the world can offer, he unconsciously—not unlike Lear—strips away all the trappings of power, position, and prestige. He arrives at the essential attribute of a man who has true identity as a man. That attribute is love. "I am certain," John Keats was to say in 1817, "of nothing but of the holiness of the Heart's affections and the truth of Imagination." The love that Antony feels for Cleopatra is not merely splendid infatuation, for infatuation could not have a quality of holiness. Because Antony's love is true, he can sacrifice all that the world can offer, and the sacrifice that he makes gives holiness to his love. In his love, Antony achieves eternal self-realization.

Thomas Thorpe was a bookseller and publisher in London during the reign of King James. In 1609, he brought out a book of one hundred and fifty-four sonnets written by Shakespeare. Most of these sonnets had probably been written several years before, some perhaps as early as 1590.

Prefixed to the sonnets is a dedication:

TO THE · ONLIE · BEGETTER · OF ·
THESE · INSUING · SONNETS,
MR. W. H., ALL HAPPINESSE
AND · THAT · ETERNITIE ·
PROMISED ·
BY ·
OUR EVER-LIVING POET ·
WISHETH ·
THE WELL-WISHING ·
ADVENTURER · IN
SETTING ·
FORTH.
T. T.

"T. T." is almost certainly Thomas Thorpe. By printing these lines with Shakespeare's poetry, he set up one of the most perplexing literary puzzles in history. That puzzle is still unsolved today. Who is "Mr. W. H."?

Of course, the identity of Mr. W. H. does not affect the quality or the beauty of the sonnets. Yet because the sonnets tell a vague and rather disconnected story, we are curious about the dedication. The story in the sonnets is one of friendship and of rivalry in love. No characters are given names, but several unnamed persons do make distinct appearances. There is a handsome young man who is urged to marry in order to perpetuate his good looks in a child. There is a rival poet. There is a "dark lady." There is "I" who is, of course, Shakespeare. The dark lady is sometimes said

125

to have been Mary Fitton, one of Queen Elizabeth's maids of honor. It has also been suggested that she may have been the Anne Whateley that Shakespeare, in 1584, had not married. Many people have thought that the rival poet was George Chapman, the author of the ill-fated *Byron* and several other plays. The handsome young man has often been identified as the Mr. W. H. of the dedication, who, it is said, may have been the Earl of Southampton. Southampton's name was Henry Wriothesley, so his initials were W. H. reversed. Also, the twenty-sixth sonnet is reminiscent of the dedication of *The Rape of Lucrece* which Shakespeare had addressed to Southampton.

There is no real proof to tell us who the characters of the sonnets are, or why Shakespeare spoke to them and about them as he did. But the sonnets are beautiful in themselves, and worthy companions to Shakespeare's plays. The most famous and the ones most often praised are the eighteenth:

Shall I compare thee to a summer's day?
Thou art more lovely and more temperate . . .

the twenty-ninth:

When, in disgrace with fortune and men's eyes,
I all alone beweep my outcast state . . .

the thirtieth:

When to the sessions of sweet silent thought
I summon up remembrance of things past . . .

126

the fifty-fifth:

> Not marble, nor the gilded monuments
> Of princes, shall outlive this powerful rhyme . . .

and the one hundred and sixteenth:

> Let me not to the marriage of true minds
> Admit impediments. Love is not love
> Which alters when it alteration finds,
> Or bends with the remover to remove:
> O, no! it is an ever fixed mark
> That looks on tempests and is never shaken;
> It is the star to every wandering bark,
> Whose worth's unknown, although his height be
>   taken.
> Love's not Time's fool, though rosy lips and
>   cheeks
> Within his bending sickle's compass come;
> Love alters not with his brief hours and weeks,
> But bears it out even to the edge of doom.
>   If this be error and upon me prov'd,
>   I never writ, nor no man ever lov'd.

Since 1590, when he had probably begun composing plays, Shakespeare had been writing with a large theater in mind. He had intended that his plays be acted before thousands of people. The stage on which his actors moved had always been a large one. Many of the speeches that he assigned to his characters were written to be spoken loudly, if not actually shouted. He had regularly included in his plays battles and

127

duels and banquets and storms. Shakespeare was very often the author of great spectacles.

Great spectacles, however, could not be presented successfully, or comfortably, in the new Blackfriars theater. It was necessary for the King's Men now to have a different kind of play. Softer, gentler pieces were needed, more suitable for presentation by candle-light to a small audience. The King's Men turned to Shakespeare. He must write several new plays. The company would, of course, continue to put on his other plays at the Globe in the summer—and, with a few alterations in staging and acting, in the winter at Blackfriars. But several plays of small dimensions were needed as well.

Shakespeare immediately set to work. He wrote *Cymbeline* probably in 1609; *The Winter's Tale* probably in 1610; and in 1611, *The Tempest*. All three have an air of serenity and calm about them that is not present in any of the major tragedies. The tragedies thunder with life and death. *Cymbeline*, *The Winter's Tale*, and *The Tempest* are the calm after the storm. In *Cymbeline*, distant low rumblings of thunder can still be heard, but by the end of the play the air has cleared. In *The Winter's Tale* and *The Tempest*, in spite of sad situations, the air is almost entirely serene. None of the three is funny, nor is any one of them really optimistic. All three seem, however, to have made their peace with the world. Life, they say, is not always gentle, not always pretty, but although it can be harsh, it is not bitter. In Shakespeare's lines of these years, we hear what

Wordsworth, nearly two centuries later, was to call "the still, sad music of humanity."

In *The Tempest*, Miranda, who has lived almost all of her life on a desert island alone with her father, sees a group of other human beings for the first time. She is just sixteen years old. She cannot restrain her affection and her enthusiasm:

> O, wonder!
> How many goodly creatures are there here!
> How beauteous mankind is! O brave new world,
> That has such people in't!

To which her father, who has seen the world, can only reply, rather sadly:

> 'Tis new to thee.

The Tempest is Shakespeare's last play. It is a short play, fifty lines shorter even than *Macbeth*. Unlike *Macbeth*, it does not give the impression of headlong motion. It is a vision, prophetic and sad, but also filled with a spirit of comfort and calm. It is music, and particularly that music of which Shelley speaks, when he says:

> Music, when soft voices die,
> Vibrates in the memory . . .

The Tempest tells the story of one remarkable day on a magic island. That day is the climax of the fortunes of all the characters in the play. Prospero and his daughter Miranda have lived on the island for twelve years. Before that, Prospero had been duke of Milan; but he had spent so much time in reading and in study that his brother Antonio had been able to seize his power from him. Prospero and Miranda had been put into a rotten boat, and pushed out to sea. They had landed on the island, and found it to be uninhabited except for Caliban, a monster, and for Ariel, a spirit, both of whom Prospero immediately makes his servants.

One day a ship passes near the island. Prospero, who is able to do such things, causes a tempest that wrecks the ship. Everyone on board is cast into the sea, but all reach shore safely. Two of the passengers are Alonso, King of Naples, and his son Ferdinand. Ferdinand meets Miranda, and immediately falls in love with her, and she with him. Another passenger is Prospero's brother, Antonio. As soon as he sets foot on land, Antonio plots with Sebastian, Ferdinand's uncle, to murder Alonso, but the plot is foiled by Ariel. Meanwhile two other passengers, Stephano and Trinculo, meet Caliban, who persuades them to try to murder Prospero. That attempt, too, fails. At the end of the play, Prospero resolves all the situations. He gives Miranda in marriage to Ferdinand. He forgives his brother, Antonio, and is promised the return of his dukedom. He sets Ariel free from servitude. Everyone then boards the ship (which magically has not been destroyed by the tempest), and it sails for Italy. Caliban is left in sole possession of the island.

Two things are immediately obvious in *The Tempest*. The first is that the play contains in miniature a recapitulation of many situations and of many types of characters that Shakespeare had used in other plays. *The Tempest* is, in one sense, a summing-up of Shakespeare's dramas, a set of variations by Shakespeare on his own themes. Prospero and Miranda remind us of King Lear and Cordelia. They are younger and more fortunate, of course, but they seem to be Lear and his daughter, held back by Shakespeare from the edge of the abyss. Ferdinand and Miranda fall in love at first sight, as did Romeo and Juliet, and Rosalind and Orlando. Although Miranda is not as worldly as either Juliet or Rosalind, Ferdinand does in many ways resemble Orlando. Antonio's plot to murder Alonso has many similarities to Macbeth's plans to murder Duncan. Ariel seems to be the Fool in *King Lear*, carried to an extreme point of development. In short, Shakespeare, wanting to write a play of limited dimensions for the smaller Blackfriars theater, seems to have—surely unconsciously—dipped into his own artistic past, and reconsidered several things that he had long been interested in. As "playing holds a mirror up to Nature," *The Tempest* holds, as it were, a mirror up to playing.

The second striking thing about *The Tempest* is the ethereal quality of the play. It is clearly make-believe, in a sense a kind of fairy tale. At the same time it is more than just an impossible fable. If it is a dream, the dream is truer than the world in which we live when we are awake. If it is a mirror image, the reflection in that mirror is truer than the reality that is reflected. *The Tempest* takes place—to use Hamlet's phrase—"between heaven and earth." In the most famous speech of the play, Prospero confirms this impression (Act IV):

Our revels now are ended. These our actors,
As I foretold you, were all spirits and
Are melted into air, into thin air:
And, like the baseless fabric of this vision,
The cloud-capp'd towers, the gorgeous palaces,
The solemn temples, the great globe itself,
Yea, all which it inherit, shall dissolve
And, like this insubstantial pageant faded,
Leave not a rack behind. We are such stuff
As dreams are made on, and our little life
Is rounded with a sleep.

Because of the ethereal quality of *The Tempest,* many readers have believed it to be a highly symbolic play. If it is symbolic, what do the characters and the situations stand for? The most frequent answer is that *The Tempest* is Shakespeare's farewell to the stage. Prospero, it is argued, is Shakespeare himself. Ariel stands for his art, his dramatic genius, which he now "sets free." The island is London; Milan is Stratford. Ferdinand and Miranda stand for Beaumont and Fletcher, who would become famous by collaborating on the writing of plays. "Our revels now are ended," says Prospero. Some readers think that Shakespeare in these lines is saying "I shall write no more."

Others, while they believe that *The Tempest* is indeed symbolic, deny that it symbolized the end of Shakespeare's career, and they also deny that Prospero is Shakespeare. After all, they argue, in none of his other plays did Shakespeare intrude his own life or thoughts into the story; why should he begin, in 1611, to dramatize himself? They believe, rather, that *The Tempest* is symbolic of church and religion. Prospero is God; Ariel is the Angel of the Lord; Caliban is the Demon; Ferdinand and Miranda are Adam and Eve; *The Tempest* is a poetical variation by Shakespeare on the story of the Garden of Eden.

Still others point out that *The Tempest* may well be an allegorical narrative of some of the events in the life of St. Carlo Borromeo, a sixteenth-century archbishop of Milan. St. Carlo was a studious and a scholarly man, as was Prospero. The civil authorities of Milan tried several times to have him turned out of office. Indeed, an assassination attempt was made on his life, as was nearly made on Prospero's life. St. Carlo, in 1577, became the hero of Milan by his bravery and his generosity during an epidemic of the plague. Not only did he fearlessly visit and help the sick, but he miraculously made the bells of a Milan church ring of their own accord. A voice spoke over the sound, saying to the citizens of the city, "I shall have pity on my people"—much as Prospero, through Ariel, makes music be heard miraculously on the island. St. Carlo also, it is said, banished the plague into a marble column—Prospero speaks of banishing Ariel (although Ariel does not stand for the plague) into a tree. The plague was, inevitably, much on Shakespeare's mind

133

in 1611, and Carlo Borromeo had been raised to sainthood in 1610. *The Tempest*, it is argued, is Shakespeare's reflection on the plague, and his tribute to a great man who had done everything humanly and miraculously possible to overcome it.

These three theories (and others have also been advanced) perhaps have a measure of truth to them. As he was writing, Shakespeare may, indeed, have noticed that unintended symbolic parallels between Prospero's life and his own had crept into his text. He may even have intentionally added one or two hints taken from his own life to the picture of Prospero. There is, however, very little reason to think that *The Tempest* is entirely a conscious allegory of Shakespeare's own life as a writer. Likewise, it is not improbable that Shakespeare may have taken one or two points from the life of St. Carlo, and incorporated them into his play. After all, the plague had raged in London again in 1609, and as Shakespeare lived through still another epidemic, his attention was attracted by the figure of one of the few Roman Catholic priests in London at the time, a certain Father Marvino, who behaved with great courage and reminded people of Carlo Borromeo. It is not surprising that Shakespeare had St. Carlo in mind as he was writing *The Tempest*; but that still does not mean that *The Tempest* is St. Carlo's biography told in allegory.

The important question is not, "What is *The Tempest* about?" but, "Why has *The Tempest*—as well as all of Shakespeare's other plays—lasted, and been loved and respected for three and a half centuries?"

One answer would be, simply, because they are works of genius.

Artistic genius is, in part at least, the artist's state of thinking and state of feeling while he is at work. Whatever the subject—a story that he is telling, a landscape that he is drawing, a piece of music that he is composing—the artist's chief consideration is for some abstract, permanent, and universal value. That consideration may be conscious or unconscious. If an artist is painting a tree, he is not only painting the tree, he is also painting the idea of creation, or the idea of growth, or the unseen roots of the tree. If he is telling the story of a beautiful woman, he is also talking about the cause or the nature of beauty as he knows it or feels it to be. The state of being of an artist of genius is involved, not with what is immediate, nor with what affects only him, but with a consideration that is eternal and is of consequence in the universal order. It has been said that Hamlet is the only character in a Shakespearian play that might have been able, theoretically, to write all the plays himself. If that idea is true, it is true in part because of Hamlet's statement to Horatio:

> There are more things in Heaven and Earth, Horatio,
> Than are dreamt of in your philosophy.

The universal consideration that, consciously or unconsciously, Shakespeare infused into *The Tempest* is the idea of consolation: "You shall be consoled." *The*

Tempest says to its readers (but not in so many words) that although life can offer storms, treachery, sorrow, violence, viciousness and pain, it can offer also consolation. That consolation, moreover, it is in man's power to provide for himself and for others. *The Tempest* is not a play of simple, smiling optimism. It is a play that says that the world need not be only a place in which there is "neither joy, nor love, nor light, nor certitude, nor peace, nor help for pain." Alleviation of sorrow is universally available to man, if he will acknowledge that it is, and study to procure it. But Shakespeare himself does not, even in this his last play, attempt to teach—in this case, teach *how* we may have that consolation and comfort. His genius simply did not work that way. Shakespeare shows us unfailingly how things are. The pictures that he paints are true. He never showed us what he himself thought ought to be changed in the world, nor ever suggested how any improvements might be made. Shakespeare is not a teacher, but a poet. We never see directly the man that held the pen.

It does not belittle *The Tempest* to point out that the conviction, arrived at in it artistically, that comfort must exist in the cosmic order, is not unique with Shakespeare's genius. It is, at the same time, true that very few artists have ever arrived at the state-of-being in which they were able to perceive and to communicate this quality. Wordsworth is among them. And at least two composers have been able to put into some pieces of their music the spirit that Shakespeare gave *The Tempest*. Bach has it in the final chorus of his *St.*

136

Matthew Passion; and Beethoven, too: in the Piano Sonata No. 32 (Opus 111) and, above all, in Opus 120, the *Diabelli Variations*.

By 1611, when he had finished writing *The Tempest*, Shakespeare was the grand old man of the London theater. For twenty years he had been acting and writing. For twenty years he had been loved and respected as a poet and a dramatist. It is no wonder that younger playwrights now turned to him, and asked for his help with the plays that they were writing. We know of at least two occasions when Shakespeare certainly gave that help.

In 1612, Shakespeare came to the aid of John Fletcher. Fletcher was fifteen years younger than Shakespeare. Fletcher also wrote for the King's Men, and had already produced several successful plays, most of them written in collaboration with Francis Beaumont. Whether, in 1612, Fletcher had started a play that he could not somehow work out to a successful conclusion; or whether Shakespeare had planned to write another play, had started it, and then, for some reason had had to abandon it, and turned what he had written over to Fletcher to finish—we cannot say. We only know that there exists a play called *The Famous History of the Life of King Henry the Eighth*, written in 1612, and it does contain some parts which are written by Shakespeare.

The next year the same thing happened again. Either Fletcher turned to Shakespeare for help, or Shakespeare had started another play but had been forced to give up the writing of it. This time the play was based on one of Chaucer's *Canterbury Tales*, and it was called *The Two Noble Kinsmen.*

The Two Noble Kinsmen was probably Shakespeare's last piece of writing of any kind. In the summer of 1613 something occurred which may have discouraged Shakespeare enough to quit the stage entirely and go back to Stratford to stay.

On June 29, 1613, a performance of *Henry VIII* was being given at the Globe. In the first act, stage directions called for the discharge of several cannon to announce the arrival of the king. Promptly on cue, after the character named Lord Sands had spoken his line

I told your Grace they would talk anon

the assistant discharged the cannon. Whether because the assistant did his work badly, or because there was a stiff breeze blowing, the Globe caught fire. Within an hour, the whole theater had burned to the ground. Luckily, no one was killed in the disaster. One man's breeches were set on fire, but another patron doused the flames with a mug of beer that he happened to be holding.

No one had been killed, but the greatest theater in the history of drama—the stage on which had first been presented *Julius Caesar, Hamlet, Othello, Macbeth, King Lear,* and others—had been reduced to ashes and rubble.

The Globe was rebuilt, and in June, 1614, the first performance was given in it. It was said to be the handsomest playhouse ever built in England. Perhaps it was. It did not, however, have as distinguished an opening as did the old Globe. Shakespeare did not write a new play especially for it.

9. Shakespeare Returns to Stratford

If Shakespeare returned to Stratford for good in 1613, with no more plans to go to London regularly for theater work, he had been away for twenty-five years. In 1588, he had left home as a young man of twenty-four with dreams of acting, writing, and making a little money with which to buy books, and to help provide for his own and his children's future. He had been completely successful. He returned to Stratford a great man—a greater man, indeed, than his neighbors realized. It might have been said of him what Hamlet had said, so quietly, but with so much love and praise, of his father:

He was a man, take him for all in all:
I shall not look upon his like again.

By 1613, Shakespeare's mother and father were both dead. His three brothers, Gilbert, Richard, and Edmund, had also died. His sister Joan was still alive, living in Stratford and bringing up her sons, William, Thomas, and Michael. Shakespeare's elder daughter Susanna was in Stratford, too, as, of course, was his grandchild. Judith, Shakespeare's younger daughter, had not married and was still living at New Place.

The town of Stratford had gradually become, during Shakespeare's lifetime, a more markedly Puritan community. Dr. Hall, Shakespeare's son-in-law, continued in his Puritan beliefs. There is, however, no record of any friction between Shakespeare and Hall, nor is it likely that Hall was able to persuade his wife to frown on her father's career. On Susanna Shakespeare Hall's gravestone (she died in 1649), it is written that she was "witty above her sex. . . . Something of Shakespeare was in that."

Still, many of the more staunchly Puritan people in Stratford must have looked upon Shakespeare as an unfortunate, and even as a sinful, man. It is hard for us to believe this today. We read some of his lines—Isabella's words in *Measure for Measure* (Act II):

> . . . But man, proud man,
> Drest in a little brief authority,
> Most ignorant of what he's most assur'd,
> His glassy essence, like an angry ape,
> Plays such fantastic tricks before high heaven
> As make the angels weep . . .

and Iago in *Othello* (Act III):

141

Good name in man and woman, dear my lord,
Is the immediate jewel of their souls:
Who steals my purse steals trash; 'tis something,
  nothing;
'Twas mine, 'tis his, and has been slave to
  thousands;
But he that filches from me my good name
Robs me of that which not enriches him,
And makes me poor indeed.

and Julius Caesar's thoughts on dying:

Cowards die many times before their deaths;
The valiant never taste of death but once.
Of all the wonders that I yet have heard,
It seems to me most strange that men should fear;
Seeing that death, a necessary end,
Will come when it will come.

—and we are filled with admiration. It is hard to believe that anyone at any time could think these words
sinful or wicked or "of the Devil's party." Yet the
Puritans found them wicked. Fashions—even those
concerned with what seem to be fundamental things—
change. What is believed sincerely today by intelligent people to be wicked, is discovered to be virtuous
tomorrow. What is thought to be pure and moral today was perhaps a sin yesterday, and may be one again
tomorrow. It is this instability of judgment, this constant uncertain swinging of the pendulum, that indirectly the artist attacks. Among other things, he

tries to find out and to reveal what is lasting and what is true. Shakespeare, in this regard, was one of the greatest artists that ever lived. What he found out, what he revealed, "what he has left us . . . was not of an age, but for all time."

In July, 1614, Stratford again was the victim of a great fire. New Place was not touched, but more than fifty houses burned to the ground, as well as the barns and stables attached to some of them. The next year history began in a sense to repeat itself for Shakespeare. His daughter Judith told him that she was engaged to be married. Her fiancé was Thomas Quiney, the son of the man that had asked Shakespeare to lend him £30 in 1598. Quiney was four years younger than Judith. Shakespeare must have been struck by the similarity, in this particular, between his daughter's marriage and his own. Whether or not Shakespeare approved of Thomas Quiney as a son-in-law, he probably did not approve of the way in which Quiney handled the wedding ceremony. Quiney persuaded the vicar to perform the marriage in February, 1616, but neglected to procure one of the documents necessary to make the marriage fully legal. As a result, the newlywed Quineys were excommunicated by the Bishop of Worcester.

Late in 1615 and early in 1616, Shakespeare drew up his will. He could not will the royalties from his plays to anyone because he had none. They had been given, or sold, outright to the Chamberlain's Men. Even so, Shakespeare had a great deal of money and property. He left to the poor of Stratford £10 (or about $1,000). He left six of his friends 26s. 8d. each (about $125) "to buy them rings." To two other friends he left somewhat larger sums of money. He left his sister the house in Henley Street, all his clothes, and £20 (about $2,000), with £5 for each of his three nephews. To his daughter Judith, he left £150 (about $14,000), and the interest on another £150; and, as well, "my broad silver gilt bowl." To his daughter Susanna, he left New Place and all his other property. And to his granddaughter Elizabeth, he left his silver.

Near the end of the will is a somewhat perplexing sentence. "I give unto my wife my second best bed with the furniture." Since this is the only mention that Shakespeare makes of his wife, it has been suggested that, perhaps because of marital discord, he had virtually cut her out of his will. But almost surely he had not. According to the law of the time, a man's widow, whether mentioned or not in his will, was legally entitled to a one-third share of all her husband's property. She was also entitled to live for the rest of her life in the house that she had shared with her husband. For this reason Shakespeare did not list his wife in his will. The fact that he left her the bed and the furniture, above her legal one-third portion, speaks of harmony rather than of discord between his wife and himself.

Shakespeare signed his will on March 25, 1616. There is no evidence that he was sick at the time. Perhaps, though, he was. On April 23, 1616, Shakespeare died. That day may have been his fifty-second birthday. The cause of his death is not known. He was buried on April 25 in Holy Trinity Church in Stratford-on-Avon. His burial was duly and briefly registered:

April 25   Will. Shakespeare gent.

10. Epilogue

Shakespeare's daughter Judith had three children, all boys. One died in infancy, one when he was twenty-one, and the third when he was nineteen. Shakespeare's daughter Susanna's only child, Elizabeth, was eight years old when her grandfather died. In 1626, she married a man named Thomas Nash, but they had no children. Nash died in 1647, and in 1649, Elizabeth was married again, this time to a certain Sir Charles Bernard. There were no children of this marriage either. Lady Elizabeth Bernard died in 1670. Her death ended the line of direct descendants of William Shakespeare.

Only two sons of Shakespeare's sister, Joan Hart, survived childhood. William followed in his uncle's footsteps and became an actor, appearing frequently at Blackfriars theater. He did not marry, and died at the age of thirty-nine. The second son, Thomas, stayed in Stratford, married, and in turn had two sons. It is from George Hart, Thomas' second son, that the only known relations of Shakespeare still living today are descended. George Hart's ninth descendant was Mr. H. G. Shakespeare Hart, who was born in 1898, and who had a daughter, born in 1940.

Seven and a half years after Shakespeare died, his plays were collected and published by two actors and shareholders in the Globe and Blackfriars companies, John Heminge and Henry Condell. The 907-page volume is known today as "The Folio." It contained a large number of typographical errors, including some misnumbering of the pages. For all of that, it gave the world the text of Shakespeare's plays. Few more valuable volumes have ever been printed.

The Puritans succeeded in keeping the theaters closed for eighteen years. When they were officially reopened in 1660, Shakespeare immediately returned to fame. Within a few years, sixteen of his plays had been performed in London theaters. In 1712, the first separate volume of analysis of Shakespeare's work appeared. It was called *On the Genius and Writings of Shakespeare* and it had been written by John Dennis. Since then, Shakespeare has been translated into virtually every language. The plays have all been acted innumerable times in nearly every country of the world. They have been studied, examined, weighed, measured, criticized, and explained by thousands of writers and scholars.

In the largest sense, though, it is true to say that Shakespeare's plays cannot be explained. A great part of what Shakespeare wrote is art, in the best and the soundest meaning of that word. Art can be studied and analyzed, and its value estimated and weighed. It cannot, however, be finally explained. Art itself is, indeed, what is lost in explanation. Life and art are closely linked. William Shakespeare the artist truly held a mirror up to Nature, and for this reason

The life ... of his lines shall never out.

Appendix A

THE ANTI-STRATFORDIANS

Some people deny that William Shakespeare, the man from Stratford, wrote the plays that bear his name. These "anti-Stratfordians" do not deny the greatness of the plays; they deny the greatness of the man. They say that a glover's son from a small country town could never have been able to produce such intricate and profound works. They admit that a William Shakespeare certainly existed but they usually argue that he merely signed his name to plays that had been written by a man who did not want his own name attached to works for the theater. After all, writing for the stage was a rather low form of occupation in Elizabethan London.

The two candidates most often proposed for "author of Shakespeare's plays" are Francis Bacon and Edward de Vere, Earl of Oxford. Other names, however, have been suggested—among them, those of Christopher Marlowe, and even of Queen Elizabeth herself.

The main argument used by most of the anti-Stratfordians revolves around Shakespeare's education. They point out that William Shakespeare of Stratford left a village grammar

149

school at the age of sixteen, and did not attend a university. While he was still young, he became an actor. In short, he received very little formal education. Shakespeare's plays, they argue, were obviously written by a man who had a vast and exact knowledge of law, medicine, geography, history, literature, religion, sports, music, and court etiquette. They point out, too, that ordinary, moderately well-educated people who speak English use no more than five thousand different words in everyday speech and writing. The author of Shakespeare's plays used eighteen thousand different words. They conclude, therefore, that the ill-educated boy from Stratford could not have grown up to become the author of these plays.

At first glance, the anti-Stratfordians may seem to have a strong point. But there are two general answers that may be made to these attacks on Shakespeare.

The first is this: that during Shakespeare's lifetime, and for one hundred and fifty years after his death, not a single voice was raised that doubted that Shakespeare was the author of "Shakespeare's plays." William Shakespeare was a famous and rich man in his own day, much in the public eye. He performed before Queen Elizabeth and King James. His name was frequently linked with his plays by many of his contemporaries. In the sixteenth and early seventeenth centuries, moreover, London was a small city. In all of England there were not half the number of people that live in London alone today. Shakespeare was easily approachable. If he had not written the plays that he said that he had, someone would sooner or later have surely discovered that fact, and would have said so. Certainly no dedicated Puritan, eager to have all drama extinguished, could have been persuaded to remain silent. Also, there were very few men at the time who had enough education, by the anti-Stratfordians' standards, to have written these plays. Francis Bacon was well educated, but he had many enemies, any one of whom would have been delighted to have linked his name publicly with "sinful" theater work. The Earl of Oxford died in 1604, and that fact

150

alone seems to rule him out as the author. It is just not very probable that the author of such famous works as Shakespeare's plays could have kept his name a secret in the London of the time.

The second answer is this: the argument that Shakespeare was incapable of writing these plays is based on a mistaken idea of the nature of genius.

Many of the anti-Stratfordians tend to think that the exquisiteness of the plays depends largely on the intellectual attainments of the man that wrote them; and, further, that education and knowledge can come only through formal study and experience. Now, there is no doubt that the author of "Shakespeare's plays" was an exceptional person. He was, indeed, so exceptional as to be barely believable. He is, for all of that, certainly not much more believable if he was Francis Bacon, than if he was the Stratford glover's son.

The author of the plays undeniably had great intellectual abilities and vast knowledge. It does not, however, follow that he must have acquired that knowledge, as most men would have, by long years of diligent study. To take a single example in a related field: Lord Macaulay knew all twelve books of Milton's *Paradise Lost* by heart, word for word. He had never, however, sat down to memorize them. In other words, Macaulay had acquired his knowledge of *Paradise Lost* by some exceptional means. Likewise, Shakespeare had an exceptional means of acquiring knowledge. He probably had a memory as prodigious as Lord Macaulay's. He remembered everything that was said to him. He memorized automatically, word for word, whole books that he had read even casually. He was able when he was writing to tap his vast memory. He was able to put into his plays names, words, whole sentences that he had read long before, or had once heard mentioned. He was able to make use of a great store of miscellaneous information that he possessed, although he had never consciously set out to acquire it. Very few men in the world have been able to do this. Shakespeare was one of

151

them. "Shakespeare's plays" are in every way extraordinary. Their author was in every way extraordinary.

For all of that, the beauty of the plays depends only in part on intellectual brilliance. Above all, they are poetry. To say that poetry can be written, or that art can be produced, only by men of great intellectual ability is to show a marked ignorance of the nature of art. The artistic expression of genius does not come from only one part of the artist: it is the expression of the whole man. In works of art, the whole is made up of the sum of its parts *plus* something else. Shakespeare's plays are the sum of the words, of the conscious and unconscious ideas that make them up—*plus* something else. That something else is art. It cannot be argued that art was available to the Earl of Oxford more than it was to William Shakespeare simply because the earl had had a better education; or, it will not be argued by anyone who has ever perceived the true greatness of Shakespeare's plays.

It is a strange fact that throughout history the identity of many famous men has often been questioned. Robin Hood, it is said, was not a stout-hearted country boy, but actually the son of the Earl of Huntingdon. King Louis XIV of France was not really the true king; the real Louis was stolen from his cradle and allowed to die in prison. Even Francis Bacon, who was supposed to have been Shakespeare, was not, according to some, actually Francis Bacon at all, but the son of Queen Elizabeth and the Earl of Leicester.

The identity of most great artists, of course, has never seriously been challenged. Beethoven, for instance, has never been challenged as the composer of his music.

We know a great deal about the life of Beethoven. We know that he had a wretched childhood during which he received a slender education. We know that as a man he was moody, argumentative, changeable, and ill-mannered. His conversation was rarely brilliant, and often silly. We know that as a relatively young man he became almost entirely deaf. We also know that in his music he gave expression to profound

152

thoughts and vigorous feelings with a brilliance, a clarity, and a variety that baffle the understanding. And we know that Beethoven wrote "Beethoven's music."

If the ill-educated and unintellectual Ludwig von Beethoven was able to compose the brilliant music that he did, then surely William Shakespeare, the country boy from Stratford-on-Avon, was able to write the plays that bear his name.

Appendix B

A LIST OF SHAKESPEARE'S PLAYS

The thirty-six plays listed in alphabetical order below are those included in the edition now known as the Folio, published in 1623. The designations of comedy, history, or tragedy given to each are those that were assigned by the original compilers of the Folio. A date of composition has been put down for each play, but it must be remembered that there is no absolute certainty about the date of any of the plays: the dates given are simply those generally accepted by most modern scholars. Some of Shakespeare's sources are also given: the poems or stories or histories that Shakespeare seems to have referred to for some of his facts, names, and general information. Finally, a plot synopsis has been included for each play not referred to in detail in the body of the book.

ALL'S WELL THAT ENDS WELL

Comedy. Date: probably 1595; revised 1603
Source: *The Decameron* (ninth tale of the third day) by Giovanni Boccaccio (1313–75).
Synopsis: Helena, a beautiful young girl, cures the King of France of a serious malady. She asks the king that, as a re-

ward, she may become the wife of Bertram, the count of Rousillon. Helena and Bertram are married but since Bertram married Helena only because of the king's command, he immediately sets out for Italy alone. Helena follows in disguise and, after many adventures, makes Bertram realize that he does, in fact, love her "dearly, ever, ever dearly."

The subplot is chiefly concerned with the doings of Parolles, a boastful and cowardly soldier in Bertram's service.

ANTONY AND CLEOPATRA

Tragedy. Date: 1607–1608
Source: The Life of Marcus Antonius in Plutarch's *Lives*.
Synopsis: See page 120.

AS YOU LIKE IT

Comedy. Date: 1599
Sources: *Rosalynde, or Euphues' Golden Legacy*, a romance by Thomas Lodge (1558?–1625); *The Tale of Gamelyn*, an anonymous poem of the fourteenth century; and, to a very slight extent, *Orlando Furioso*, an epic poem by Lodovico Ariosto (1474–1533).
Synopsis: See page 60.

THE COMEDY OF ERRORS

Comedy. Date: 1593
Sources: *Menaechmi* and *Amphitruo* by Titus Maccius Plautus (254–184 B.C.).
Synopsis: Syracuse and Ephesus are enemy cities. Aegeon and Aemilia of Syracuse have identical twin sons, both of whom are called Antipholus, and both of whom have identical twin attendants, both called Dromio. The members of this household are separated from one another by a shipwreck, and many years are spent by one Antipholus and one Dromio in looking for the other Antipholus and the other Dromio.

Aegeon, in turn, is looking for the son who is looking for the other son. In the meantime, the "other son" has married a girl named Adriana. All of these people find themselves in Ephesus on the same day, where inevitably the Antipholuses and the Dromios are confused, with embarrassing results. Aegeon risks being executed because he is a Syracusan within the domains of Ephesus. A scene of general recognition and pardon concludes the play.

CORIOLANUS

Tragedy. Date: 1608

Sources: The Life of Caius Marcius Coriolanus in Plutarch's *Lives*.

Synopsis: Caius Marcius, a Roman general, is offered the consulship and also the surname "Coriolanus" in return for his brave exploits in a battle against Corioli, a Volscian town. The common people, however, soon find that they do not like some things about Coriolanus and, urged on by a number of jealous tribunes, demand that he be banished. Coriolanus then joins his earlier Volscian opponent, Aufidius, and leads an army against Rome. He is persuaded by his mother, his wife, and his son to spare Rome, and he returns to Corioli. There he is murdered by an enraged and jealous Aufidius.

CYMBELINE

Tragedy. Date: 1609–10

Sources: *The Decameron* (II, ix); *The Rare Triumphs of Love and Fortune,* an anonymous play written before 1589; and *The Chronicles of England, Scotland, and Ireland* by Raphael Holinshed (1529?–1580?).

Synopsis: Posthumus has secretly married Imogen, daughter of Cymbeline, King of Britain. This marriage displeases the queen (Cymbeline's second wife) because she had hoped for a marriage between Imogen and her son, Cloten. She reveals all to Cymbeline, and Posthumus is banished. In Rome,

Posthumus makes a bet with Iachimo that Imogen will remain absolutely faithful to him. Iachimo goes to Britain, hides in a trunk and thus gets into Imogen's room. During the night, he comes out of the trunk, notes as many particulars about Imogen's room as he can, and manages to get back to Rome, where he makes his perfidious report to Posthumus. Convinced that Imogen has been unfaithful, Posthumus orders his servant Pisanio to murder her. Pisanio, however, does not commit the murder; and Imogen, disguised as a man, joins the army of Lucius, a Roman general who is invading Britain. Imogen meets Belarius and his two sons: but Belarius' sons are really Cymbeline's sons and Imogen's brothers, who had been stolen by Belarius when they were babies. Cloten is killed by Imogen's brothers. The Roman army is defeated, partly through the bravery of Posthumus, who secretly has returned out of banishment. A scene of recognition and general reconciliation closes the play.

HAMLET

Tragedy. Date: 1600–1601
Sources: *Historia Danica* by Saxo Grammaticus (1150?–1206), rendered into French and included in *Histoires Tragiques* by François de Belleforest (1530–83); a play on the subject of Hamlet, now lost, and usually referred to as *Ur-Hamlet*.
Synopsis: See page 80.

HENRY IV, PART ONE

History. Date: 1596–97
Sources: Holinshed's *Chronicles*; *The First Four Books of the Civil Wars between the Two Houses of Lancaster and York*, an epic poem by Samuel Daniel; and *The Famous Victories of Henry V*, an anonymous play written before 1594.

Synopsis: The Earl of Northumberland and his son, Henry (who is called Hotspur), with several other persons, mount an open rebellion against King Henry IV. At the battle of Shrewsbury, Hotspur is killed by the Prince of Wales (Prince Hal), and the rebellion is put down. Much of the play deals with the deeds and misdeeds of Sir John Falstaff, a decayed, humorous, fat, and amiable middle-aged knight, who is a friend of Prince Hal's.

HENRY IV, PART TWO

History. Date: 1597–98
Sources: See *Henry IV, Part One*.
Synopsis: Richard Scroop, Archbishop of York, Lord Mowbray, and Lord Hastings plot against King Henry IV. King Henry's third son, Prince John, meets the rebels and promises to redress their grievances; but after they have laid down their arms, he has them taken prisoner and executed. King Henry dies, and Prince Hal ascends the throne as King Henry V. One of his first acts is to reprove Sir John Falstaff for his general misbehavior; and Falstaff is sent to prison by the Chief Justice.

HENRY V

History. Date: 1599
Sources: Holinshed's *Chronicles*, and *The Famous Victories of Henry V*.
Synopsis: King Henry V is encouraged by the Archbishop of Canterbury to invade France and seize the French throne. Before setting out, King Henry discovers and thwarts a plot to assassinate him. In France, Henry's army engages the French forces at Agincourt and defeats them. King Charles of France accepts the English terms for peace: according to them, King Henry marries Katharine, King Charles' daughter, and is declared heir to the throne of France.

The subplot is concerned chiefly with three unsavory characters named Pistol, Bardolph, and Nym. Bardolph and Nym are hanged for looting, but Pistol returns to England having promised himself to spend the rest of his days in a life of crime.

HENRY VI, PART ONE

History. Date: 1591?

Sources: *The Union of the Noble and Illustre Famelies of Lancaster and York* by Edward Halle (1498?–1547), and Holinshed's *Chronicles*.

Synopsis: On the death of King Henry V, his son becomes King Henry VI although he is still an infant. The English positions in France are threatened, mainly through the political and military ability of Joan of Arc. Lord Talbot, the most able of the English military leaders, is killed in battle. Joan of Arc is captured by the English under the Duke of York and is sentenced to be burned. Henry VI makes plans to marry Margaret, the daughter of the Duke of Anjou.

HENRY VI, PART TWO

History. Date: 1590?

Sources: See *Henry VI, Part One.*

Synopsis: The Duke of Suffolk, entrusted with the arrangement of the marriage between King Henry and Margaret, and partly because he is himself in love with the king's bride-to-be, cedes the territory of Maine and Anjou to Margaret's father. The Duke of Gloucester, King Henry's uncle, is angered by what Suffolk has done and he goes so far as to cast doubts on Suffolk's loyalty. Gloucester's enemies succeed in having the Duchess of Gloucester banished, and finally Gloucester himself is arrested and murdered. The Duke of Suffolk is banished and killed. The play ends with the opening of the Wars of the Roses: the king's forces are defeated at the battle of St. Albans.

HENRY VI, PART THREE

History. Date: 1590–91?

Sources: See *Henry VI, Part One*.

Synopsis: After the battle of St. Albans, King Henry disinherits Edward, his son, and names the Duke of York his heir; but Queen Margaret is determined to protect Edward's right to the throne. The Duke of York is seized and murdered; his sons, Edward and Richard, defeat Henry in battle, and Edward mounts the throne as King Edward IV. York's son Richard, Duke of Gloucester, is very eager to become king himself. King Edward displeases many people by his marriage to Lady Elizabeth Grey. At the battle of Tewkesbury, Queen Margaret's forces are defeated, and her son Edward is stabbed to death. The Duke of Gloucester murders Henry VI in the Tower of London.

HENRY VIII

History. Date: 1612–13

Sources: Holinshed's *Chronicles*, and *Actes and Monuments* (popularly known as *The Book of Martyrs*) by John Foxe (1516–87).

Synopsis: Cardinal Wolsey presses a charge of treason against the Duke of Buckingham, and Buckingham is tried and executed. Queen Katharine is divorced, and King Henry marries Anne Bullen (or Boleyn). Cardinal Wolsey, who opposes the marriage between the king and Anne Bullen, is disgraced and dies. A daughter is born to the king and his new queen; she is christened Elizabeth.

JULIUS CAESAR

Tragedy. Date: 1599

Sources: The Life of Julius Caesar, the Life of Marcus Brutus, and the Life of Marcus Antonius in Plutarch's *Lives*.

Synopsis: See page 76.

KING JOHN

History. Date: 1596?

Source: *The Troublesome Reign of John, King of England,* an anonymous play, written before 1591.

Synopsis: The King of France and the Duke of Austria support the claim of Arthur, nephew of King John of England, to the English throne. An attempt to arrange a peace between England and France fails. The English are victorious in battle. Philip, the illegitimate son of Richard the Lion-Hearted (King John's brother and once King of England), kills the Duke of Austria; Arthur is captured, and word is given out that he is dead. Constance, Arthur's mother, dies of grief at the news, and Arthur kills himself while trying to escape his captors. King John is suspected of complicity in Arthur's death; he is poisoned and dies, leaving the throne to his son, Henry, who becomes King Henry III.

KING LEAR

Tragedy. Date: 1606

Sources: *The True Chronicle History of King Leir and his three daughters, Gonorill, Ragan and Cordella,* an anonymous play, written before 1594; Holinshed's *Chronicles*; and the *Essays* by Michel de Montaigne, translated into English in 1603 by John Florio.

Synopsis: See page 111.

LOVE'S LABOUR'S LOST

Comedy. Date: 1594

Source: The plot seems to have been of Shakespeare's invention, although many of the characters in the play were modeled on persons that were alive and well known in France in the early 1590's.

Synopsis: Ferdinand, King of Navarre, and his attending lords, Berowne, Longaville, and Dumaine, vow to study for three years and to avoid the company of all women during that time. In spite of this plan, the king falls in love with the Princess of France, and each of the three lords falls in love with one of the ladies attending on the princess. News comes, however, of the death of the princess' father. All four ladies depart, but before they leave, they promise to marry their suitors within the year.

The subplot concerns Holofernes, a schoolmaster; Nathaniel, a curate; and the love that both Don Armado, "a fantastical Spaniard," and Costard, a clown, feel for Jaquenetta.

MACBETH

Tragedy. Date: 1606
Sources: Holinshed's *Chronicles*, which, for their Scottish material, seem to have drawn on the work of such scholars and historians as Hector Boece (1465?–1536) and Andrew of Wyntoun (1350–1420).
Synopsis: See page 105.

MEASURE FOR MEASURE

Comedy. Date: 1604
Sources: *Promos and Cassandra*, a play written in 1578 by George Whetstone. Whetstone based his play on a story that he found in a collection of tales entitled *Hecatommithi*, written by Giovanni Battista Giraldi (known as "Cinzio"), in 1565.
Synopsis: The Duke of Vienna turns over his power and authority to Angelo and to Escalus and, although he pretends to leave, really stays in Vienna disguised as a monk. Angelo proves a stern ruler: he condemns to death a young man named Claudio, because Claudio's fiancée is about to have a child by him though they are not yet married. Angelo also proves a hypocrite and a liar: he promises to spare Claudio if Isabella, Claudio's sister, agrees to become his mistress for

a night. Isabella refuses, but the duke, still in disguise, manages to arrange matters so that Claudio's life is saved anyway. At the end of the play, the duke returns out of disguise, pardons Angelo, and proposes marriage to Isabella.

The subplot deals with the actions and the antics of Lucio and Pompey and Mistress Overdone and several other members of Vienna low-life.

THE MERCHANT OF VENICE

Comedy. Date: 1597

Sources: *The Decameron* (X, i); *Il Pecorone* (a collection of tales) by Ser Giovanni Fiorentino (the first tale of the fourth day); and perhaps some of the events in the life of Dr. Roderigo Lopez, a physician to Queen Elizabeth. He was hanged in 1594 on the charge—probably unfounded—of having plotted to poison his royal patient.

Synopsis: See page 74.

THE MERRY WIVES OF WINDSOR

Comedy. Date: 1598

Sources: The plot seems to have been of Shakespeare's invention, although the theme of the play appears in a number of folktales and forms the subject of not a few anecdotes. Some of the particular persons and events were undoubtedly modeled on persons and events well known in Shakespeare's day.

Synopsis: Falstaff (see *Henry IV, Part One*) writes love letters to the wife of Page and the wife of Ford. As a result, Falstaff finds himself thrown into the river Thames, while concealed in a basket of dirty laundry, and later finds himself being beaten by Ford, who has taken him for a witch. Page's daughter, Anne, manages to elope with Fenton, the man that she loves; and her other two suitors are tricked into eloping with boys disguised as girls.

A MIDSUMMER NIGHT'S DREAM

Comedy. Date: 1595–96

Sources: The plot seems to have been of Shakespeare's invention. He probably, however, made some use of both the Life of Theseus in Plutarch's *Lives* and *The Knight's Tale* by Geoffrey Chaucer.

Synopsis: Theseus and Hippolyta are to be married. Bottom and some other Athenian workmen are preparing, in the woods near Athens, a performance of "Pyramus and Thisbe" by way of celebration of the marriage. Lysander and Hermia run away together and get to the woods, and so do Demetrius, who is in love with Hermia, and Helena, who is in love with Demetrius. Oberon, the fairy king, puts a magic juice on the eyes of Titania, the fairy queen; as a result she falls in love with the first person that she sees when she wakes up: and that happens to be Bottom, whose head, however, has been turned into the head of an ass by Oberon's servant, Puck. The magic love juice is then used rather liberally, and several people find themselves in love with people that they do not love. Finally the spells are all removed. Lysander marries Hermia; Demetrius marries Helena; and the performance of "Pyramus and Thisbe" is given.

MUCH ADO ABOUT NOTHING

Comedy. Date: 1598–99

Sources: The Claudio-Hero plot: *Orlando Furioso* (Cantos IV-VI) by Lodovico Ariosto; *Novelle* (Tale XXII) by Matteo Bandello; and *The Faerie Queene* (II, iv) by Edmund Spenser. The Beatrice-Benedick plot seems to have been of Shakespeare's invention.

Synopsis: Don John arranges matters so that Claudio thinks that he sees Hero, the woman that he loves, being made love to by another man. Claudio denounces Hero in church. She faints; and it is said that she is dead. Claudio discovers that he has been duped, and he and Hero are married.

The subplot deals with Benedick, who professes to be a confirmed bachelor, and Beatrice, who says that she will never marry. They are each tricked into believing that the other is in love; and finally, both in fact deeply in love with each other, they make arrangements to be married.

OTHELLO

Tragedy. Date: 1604
Source: *Hecatommithi* (seventh tale of the third decade) by Cinzio.
Synopsis: See page 93.

RICHARD II

History. Date: 1595
Source: Holinshed's *Chronicles*.
Synopsis: King Richard banishes both Henry Bolingbroke and Thomas Mowbray. Bolingbroke's father, John of Gaunt, dies, and Richard seizes his property in order to meet the expenses of a war that he is fighting in Ireland. Bolingbroke returns illegally out of banishment with the declared intention of getting back his father's property. It turns out, however, that many in England besides Bolingbroke are dissatisfied with Richard's kingship. Richard finds himself all but deserted. He gives up the crown to Bolingbroke, who ascends the throne as King Henry IV. Richard is taken to prison and there is murdered.

RICHARD III

History. Date: 1592
Sources: Holinshed's *Chronicles; The Union of the Noble and Illustre Famelies of Lancaster and York* by Edward Halle. Halle, in turn, seems to have drawn on *The Life of Richard*

165

III by Sir Thomas More (1478–1535) and on *Historia Anglica* by Polydore Vergil (1470?–1555).

Synopsis: Richard, Duke of Gloucester and brother of King Edward IV, declares that he is "determined to prove a villain." He is also determined to become king. Richard has his brother Clarence murdered and he marries Lady Anne, who had been the fiancée of Henry VI's murdered son. When King Edward dies, Richard, encouraged by the Duke of Buckingham, attacks those that are friendly to Edward's widow and children; and he has himself proclaimed king. Then he has Edward's two sons murdered and he makes plans to strengthen his position by marrying the daughter of his brother's widow by her first husband. But Henry Tudor, Earl of Richmond, sends an army against Richard. Richard is defeated at Bosworth Field and killed by Richmond, who then becomes King Henry VII.

ROMEO AND JULIET

Tragedy. Date: 1595

Sources: *The Tragicall Historye of Romeus and Iuliet* by Arthur Brooke (? –1563). Brooke may have taken particulars for his story from *The Divine Comedy* (Purg. vi) by Dante Alighieri (1265–1321); from *Il Novellino* by Masuccio Salernitano (1415?–1477?); from Matteo Bandello's *Novelle* (II, 9); and from *The Palace of Pleasure* by William Painter (1540?-1594).

Synopsis: Two rich and powerful families in the city of Verona, the Montagues and the Capulets, have long been, and are now, carrying on a feud. In spite of this, young Romeo Montague falls in love with Juliet Capulet, who is not quite fourteen years old. Romeo and Juliet are secretly married by Friar Lawrence. Very soon afterward Romeo kills Tybalta, Capulet, in the course of a feud-inspired brawl. Juliets' father, in the meantime, orders his daughter to marry Paris, a rich young nobleman of Verona. Friar Lawrence tries to help the wretched newlywed couple. He persuades Romeo to go to the neighboring city of Mantua; and he gives Juliet a magic potion that will make it appear to everyone that she is dead. Juliet drinks the potion and is duly buried in the family vault. But Friar Lawrence's message to Romeo in Mantua miscarries: Friar John, the messenger, was detained in Verona by regulations designed to combat an outbreak of the plague. Romeo hears that Juliet is dead and he knows nothing of the magic potion. He goes to Verona, drinks poison and dies beside Juliet. Juliet awakes, sees Romeo dead, and stabs herself. The Montagues and the Capulets are reconciled, finally, in the face of the tragedy that so grieves both families.

THE TAMING OF THE SHREW

Comedy. Date: 1594

Sources: *The Taming of a Shrew*, an anonymous play written before 1594; and *Supposes*, a comedy by George Gascoigne (1530?–1577), who, in turn, had drawn on *I suppositi*, a comedy by Lodovico Ariosto (1474–1533).

Synopsis: Christopher Sly, a drunken tinker, is found asleep on a heath by a lord returning from a hunt. The lord takes Sly to his castle and plays a trick on him: he persuades him that he really is a nobleman, who has been out of his mind for fifteen years. He provides him with a wife (who is really a page in disguise), and a company of traveling players give a performance of ''a pleasant comedy'' to try to help banish his malady.

The ''comedy'' concerns Baptista of Padua, who has two daughters: Katharina and Bianca. Katharina is a shrew. Baptista declares that Katharina shall be married before he will consent to Bianca's being married. Petruchio presents himself as a suitor for Kate. He marries her and, having taken her to his country house, tames her and cures her of her shrewishness by not allowing her either to eat or to sleep. In the meantime, Petruchio's friend, Hortensio, loses

Bianca to Lucentio but he consoles himself by marrying a rich widow. At the end of the play, there is a feast in Lucentio's house. Petruchio wagers that his Kate, the former shrew, is the most obedient and submissive of the three wives. He wins the wager.

THE TEMPEST

Comedy. Date: **1611**
Sources: A letter to an unnamed "Excellent Lady in England" written in 1610 by William Strachey, in which he describes the wreck of the *Sea-Venture* on Bermuda; perhaps *Die Schöne Sidea*, a comedy by Jakob Ayrer (? –1605); *Of The Cannibals* by Michel de Montaigne, and translated in 1603 by John Florio; and many other compositions. Scholars are not in agreement on exactly what the full sources of *The Tempest* are.
Synopsis: See page 129.

TIMON OF ATHENS

Tragedy. Date: 1605? 1606? 1607?
Sources: Passages in the Life of Antonius and the Life of Alcibiades in Plutarch's *Lives*; and *Timon the Misanthrope*, a dialogue by Lucian (120?–180?).
Synopsis: Timon, a rich and noble Athenian, gives money and presents liberally to many of his friends and acquaintances. He does not curb his generosity, despite the jibes of Apemantus or the warnings given him by his faithful steward that his enormous fortune has dwindled to nothing. When Timon's money is exhausted, he tries to borrow some from several of the persons toward whom he has been most generous. They all refuse his request. Timon then gives one last sumptuous banquet for all his supposed friends but at it he serves merely stones and bowls of warm water. After the banquet, Timon retires to a cave near Athens. There he lives on roots and he accidentally discovers gold, which wrath-

fully he gives away to anyone who happens to pass his way. Some members of the Athenian senate come to his cave to try to persuade him to return to civilization and to join in the effort to defeat Alcibiades, who is determined to overthrow Athens by force of arms. Timon refuses this request. Alcibiades takes Athens; and it is reported that Timon is dead.

TITUS ANDRONICUS

Tragedy. Date: 1592?

Sources: *Troades* and *Thyestes* by Lucius Annaeus Seneca (4 B.C.?–A.D. 65); *Metamorphoses* (Book VI) by Ovid (Publius Ovidius Naso) (43 B.C.–A.D. 17).

Synopsis: Titus Andronicus is victorious over the Goths and returns to Rome with several captives, including Tamora, Queen of the Goths. Saturninus is elected emperor and he plans to marry Lavinia, Titus' daughter. Bassianus, Saturninus' brother, however, carries off Lavinia, and Saturninus marries Tamora. Tamora, aided by Aaron, her lover, plots her revenge. Bassianus is murdered. Lavinia is ravished, her hands are cut off, and her tongue is cut out. Titus' sons, Quintus and Martius, are also murdered. Titus manages to learn from Lavinia who has ravished her; and, with his brother, Marcus, and his remaining son, Lucius, in turn plots his revenge. He gives a banquet, and at the banquet serves a pie made from the flesh of Tamora's sons. He then kills Lavinia, to put an end to her agony and her dishonor, and next kills Tamora. Saturninus kills Titus, and Lucius kills Saturninus. Lucius becomes emperor and orders the torture and execution of Aaron.

TROILUS AND CRESSIDA

Tragedy. (When published in 1609, in Quarto, *Troilus and Cressida* was described as a history.) Date: 1601–1602

Sources: *Troilus and Criseyde* by Geoffrey Chaucer, who

based his poem on *Filostrato* by Giovanni Boccaccio. Shakespeare doubtless referred back to his own *The Rape of Lucrece* (lines 1366–1561). The background of the play is that originally described in Homer's *Iliad*.

Synopsis: Calchas has deserted Troy for the Greeks. Troilus is in love with Calchas' daughter, Cressida, who lives with her uncle, Pandarus. The two lovers meet; but Calchas arranges that Cressida is to be exchanged for a Trojan prisoner, and Diomedes is sent to conduct Cressida to the Greek camp. Troilus' brother, Hector, sends a challenge to single combat to the Greeks. Achilles is the Greek champion but he is sulking in his tent and refuses to fight. Hector fights the Greek, Ajax, but their combat is short and to no decision. Achilles, however, rouses himself to insult Hector and to promise to fight with him the next day. Troilus discovers that Cressida has been unfaithful to him with Diomedes and is heartbroken. Achilles kills Hector.

TWELFTH NIGHT

Comedy. Date: 1601–1602
Sources: *Apolonius and Silla* by Barnabe Rich (1540?–1617). Rich drew on one of the *Novelle* by Matteo Bandello, who had, in turn, probably drawn on *Gl'Ingannati*, an anonymous comedy produced in Siena in 1531. The subplot (the Malvolio–Sir Toby Belch–Sir Andrew Aguecheek story) seems to have been of Shakespeare's own invention.
Synopsis: See page 64.

THE TWO GENTLEMEN OF VERONA

Comedy. Date: 1594
Source: *La Diana Enamorada* by Jorge de Montemayor (1521?–1561), translated from the Spanish into French in 1578 and into English, by Bartholomew Yonge in 1582.
Synopsis: Valentine and Proteus are the two gentlemen.

Valentine goes to Milan and falls in love with the duke's daughter, Silvia. Proteus wants to stay in Verona, in order to be near Julia, the girl that he loves, but his father sends him to Milan. In Milan, Proteus, too, falls in love with Silvia and manages to have Valentine banished. Julia disguises herself as a boy named Sebastian, comes to Milan and discovers Proteus making love to Silvia. Silvia rejects Proteus and, afraid that her father will force her to marry a rich suitor named Thurio, runs away to find Valentine. Proteus and Sebastian follow her and rescue her from some outlaws, whose honest captain is Valentine. Sebastian reveals her identity. Proteus understands that he loves her better than he does Silvia; the outlaws are pardoned by the duke; and Silvia is to marry her Valentine.

THE WINTER'S TALE

Comedy. Date: 1610?–1611

Sources: *Pandosto, or Dorastus and Fawnia* by Robert Greene (1558–92); and *Metamorphoses* by Ovid (43 B.C.–A.D. 17).

Synopsis: Leontes, the King of Sicilia, is convinced that his wife, Hermione, has been unfaithful to him with Polixenes. Thus, when Hermione gives birth to a daughter, Leontes orders that the infant be left in "some remote and desert place." Not long afterward, it is announced to Leontes that Hermione, and Mamillius, Leontes' and Hermione's son, are dead. A shepherd in Bohemia finds the baby girl and brings her up as his daughter. Her name becomes Perdita. When she is sixteen, Florizel, Polixenes' son, falls in love with her; but Polixenes forbids the marriage. Perdita and Florizel run away from Bohemia to Sicilia. There Leontes discovers that Perdita is his daughter; a statue of Hermione shown to Leontes proves to be Hermione herself, who has been living in secret retirement for all these years; the quarrel between Polixenes and Leontes is made up; and plans are made for the marriage of Florizel and Perdita.

PLAYS NOT IN THE FOLIO BUT
OCCASIONALLY ATTRIBUTED TO SHAKESPEARE

Pericles, Prince of Tyre: This play, written probably in 1608, is generally thought today to have been, in large part, by Shakespeare. George Wilkins, of whose life little is known, published a novel entitled *The Painfull Aduentures of Pericles Prince of Tyre* . . . in 1608, and may have collaborated with Shakespeare on the play. *Pericles* was published in 1609 in Quarto with Shakespeare's name on the title page. It is the only one of the "doubtful plays" included today in most editions of the complete works of Shakespeare.

The London Prodigal: Published in 1605, with Shakespeare's name on the title page, and reprinted in the Third Folio (second edition, 1664) of Shakespeare's works, this play is now generally thought by most scholars not to have been even in part by Shakespeare.

Thomas Lord Cromwell: The title page of the first edition of this play (1602) contains the words "Written by W. S." Most scholars, with the prominent exception of August Wilhelm von Schlegel (1767–1845), are unanimously in agreement that the play is not by Shakespeare, although it was included in the Third Folio. The author may have been Wentworth Smith, of whose life little is known.

Sir John Oldcastle: A play in two parts, the second part of which has been lost. Although the first part was printed in the Third Folio, there is nearly universal agreement that it was not, in fact, the work of Shakespeare.

The Puritan (sometimes known as *The Puritan Widow*): Originally published (1607) with the phrase "Written by W. S." on the title page and included in the Third Folio, this play is almost surely not by Shakespeare, but may have been one of the works of Wentworth Smith.

172

A Yorkshire Tragedy: Published in 1608, with the phrase "Written by W. Shakespeare" on the title page, this play is no longer thought to have been written by Shakespeare largely because its style is more crude and uneven than is the style of Shakespeare's work after the early 1590's. *A Yorkshire Tragedy* is, however, a powerful play. Shakespeare may have worked with its author (who was perhaps Thomas Heywood) on its composition.

Locrine: The words "Newly set forth, overseen and corrected, by W. S." appeared on the title page of this play when it was first published in 1595. The "W. S." in this case may have been William Smith, the author of a sonnet sequence entitled *Chloris*. It is not probable that Shakespeare had anything at all to do with this play. It was, however, included in the Third Folio.

The Two Noble Kinsmen: Most scholars believe that Shakespeare collaborated with John Fletcher on this play. (See page 137.

Cardenio: The entire text of this play has been lost. It has been thought by some scholars to have been the work of Shakespeare and John Fletcher in collaboration, and written between the years 1611 and 1613. A play entitled *Cardenio* (or *Cardenno*, or *Cardenna*) is known to have been acted by the King's Men in 1613.

Sir Thomas More: This play is the most tantalizing of all the "doubtful plays." A thirty-two-page manuscript copy of it exists (although the manuscript is in bad disrepair), and of these pages, three are thought by many scholars to be in Shakespeare's hand. The conclusions reached by modern scholarship are, briefly, these: that the play was the work of several authors in collaboration, and these original authors were probably Anthony Munday, Henry Chettle, and Thomas Heywood; that the work of these three men was then revised by two other writers, Thomas Dekker and Shakespeare. In any case, five different handwritings can easily be identified in the manuscript. Handwriting "D" is that usually said to be Shakespeare's, in that graphologists agree that handwriting "D" and signatures extant and known to be Shakespeare's are by the same person. Literary critics have found evidence that the imagery, the thought, and the general tone of the lines written in handwriting "D" are markedly Shakespearian. The spelling of certain words written in handwriting "D" corresponds to spellings evidently favored by Shakespeare. On the other hand, it has been argued that scholars have identified "D" as Shakespeare because, unconsciously, they want to have a specimen of Shakespeare's hand and so have allowed themselves to find what they set out to look for. In any case, the play was censored by Edmund Tilney, Master of the Revels (see page 31) both when it was first submitted to him and when it was submitted the second time, revised by Dekker and by Shakespeare—if they, indeed, were the revisers.

Edward III: This anonymous play was first published in 1596. Certain eminent persons have been convinced—the scholars Capell, A. W. Ward, and Fleay, as well as Lord Tennyson, among them—that at least Act II of the work is Shakespearian. As well, the line

Lilies that fester smell far worse than weeds
occurs in Act II, Scene i, of this play and is also the last line of Shakespeare's sonnet 94. It may be that Shakespeare started, but did not finish, a revision of the play. It seems to be all but certain that it was not his work, in its entirety or even in large part.

Fair Em, Mucedorus, and *The Merry Devil of Edmonton*: These three plays, bound and labeled "Shakespeare. Vol. I" were found in the library of King Charles II of England. Most scholars agree, however, that none of the three, in part or in its entirety, is by Shakespeare.

Appendix C

A SHORT BIBLIOGRAPHY

The Complete Works of William Shakespeare, edited with a glossary by W. J. Craig. London: Oxford University Press, 1905 (reprinted at frequent intervals).

The Complete Works of Shakespeare, edited by George Lyman Kittredge. Boston: Ginn and Company, 1936. Kittredge includes *The Two Noble Kinsmen*, which Craig omitted; and omits the *Six Sonnets to Sundry Notes of Music*, which Craig included.

The Complete Works of Shakespeare, edited by Hardin Craig. Chicago: Scott, Foresman and Company, 1951 (several times reprinted). This edition contains a great deal of biographical, historical, and critical material.

The two best-known series of single editions of the plays are:

The Arden Edition of the Works of William Shakespeare. London: Methuen & Co., Ltd.

The New Cambridge Shakespeare. Cambridge: Cambridge University Press.

Adams, J. Q. *A Life of William Shakespeare.* New York: Houghton Mifflin Co., 1923.

Bentley, Gerald Eades. *Shakespeare: A Biographical Handbook.* New Haven: Yale University Press, 1961.

Bradley, A. C. *Shakespearean Tragedy.* London: 1904; London: Macmillan & Co., Ltd., 1950 (and several times further reprinted). One of the standard pieces of criticism on tragedy in general, and on *Hamlet, Othello, King Lear,* and *Macbeth* in particular. Bradley's analysis of *Antony and Cleopatra* is published in a collection of essays entitled *Oxford Lectures on Poetry* (Bloomington: Indiana University Press, 1961).

Brown, Ivor. *How Shakespeare Spent the Day.* London: The Bodley Head, Ltd., 1963. Interesting and informative.

Campbell, Oscar James, editor, and Quinn, Edward G., associate editor. *The Reader's Encyclopedia of Shakespeare.* New York: Thomas Y. Crowell Company, 1966. A 1014-page volume containing facts and opinions on very nearly every aspect of Shakespeare's life and works and literary and dramatic fortunes. Major articles have been contributed by such scholars as Muriel St. Clare Byrne, Alfred Harbage, Clifford Leech, Louis Marder, Allardyce Nicoll, and Mario Praz. A balanced and valuable book.

Chambers, Sir E. K. *The Elizabethan Stage.* Oxford: The Clarendon Press, 1923.

Charlton, H. B. *Shakespearean Tragedy.* Cambridge: Cambridge University Press, 1948.

Chute, Marchette. *Shakespeare of London.* New York: E. P. Dutton & Co., 1949.

Coleridge, Samuel Taylor. *Lectures on Shakespeare.* London: Everyman's Library, J. M. Dent & Sons, Ltd., 1907 (many times reprinted; found in several editions and several anthologies).

de Banke, Cécile. *Shakespearean Stage Production Then and Now.* New York: McGraw-Hill, Inc., 1953. An informative work on Elizabethan and modern techniques of costume, staging, lighting, and the like.

Dowden, Edward. *Shakespere—His Mind and Art.* New York: G. P. Putnam's Sons (Capricorn Books), 1962.

Written in 1875, this book continues to be of interest and of value.

Fripp, E. I. *Shakespeare, Man and Artist*. London: Oxford University Press, 1938.

Halliday, F. E. *A Shakespeare Companion*. New York: Funk & Wagnalls Company, Inc., 1952 (and reprinted). A 750-page dictionary of information on Shakespeare's life and times and works, and on Shakespearian criticism and productions of Shakespeare's plays, by one of the twentieth century's most balanced and erudite scholars.

———— *The Life of Shakespeare*. London: Penguin Books, Inc., 1961. A short, balanced, and interesting life of Shakespeare that contains as well some sound remarks on the plays and poems.

Harbage, Alfred. *As They Liked It*. New York: Harper, 1961.

———— *Conceptions of Shakespeare*. Cambridge: Harvard University Press, 1966.

———— *Shakespeare's Audience*. New York: Columbia University Press, 1941.

Hazlitt, William. *Characters of Shakespear's Plays*. London: Everyman's Library, J. M. Dent & Sons, Ltd., 1906 (and many times reprinted).

Jones, Ernest. *Hamlet and Oedipus*. New York: Doubleday, 1954. The psychoanalyst's approach to *Hamlet*. A well-written book that is at its most persuasive when the author is not dealing with his chosen theme.

Knight, G. Wilson. *The Wheel of Fire*, 4th edition. London: Methuen, 1960.

———— *The Imperial Theme*, 3rd edition. London: Methuen, 1961.

———— *The Shakespearean Tempest*, 3rd edition. London: Methuen, 1953.

———— *The Crown of Life*. London: Methuen, 1958. All four of the foregoing are volumes of criticism of the plays.

Levin, Harry. *The Question of Hamlet*. New York: Oxford University Press, 1959.

Marder, Louis. *His Exits and His Entrances: The Story of*

Shakespeare's Reputation. Philadelphia: J. B. Lippincott Company, 1963.

Murry, John Middleton. *Shakespeare.* London: Jonathan Cape, Ltd., 1936 (and reprinted). A book about all of Shakespeare's writings by a sensitive and well-read man. The book as a whole is perhaps somewhat subjective but it contains many vivid and penetrating ideas.

Neilson, W. A., and Thorndike, A. H. *The Facts About Shakespeare.* New York: The Macmillan Company, 1961 (and reprinted).

Quennell, Peter. *Shakespeare.* New York: Avon Books, 1963.

Raleigh, Walter. *Shakespeare.* London: Macmillan & Co., Ltd., 1957 (and reprinted).

Sitwell, Edith. *A Notebook on Shakespeare.* London: Macmillan & Co., Ltd., 1948.

Spencer, Theodore. *Shakespeare and the Nature of Man.* New York: The Macmillan Company, 1942 (and reprinted).

Wilson, J. Dover. *The Fortunes of Falstaff.* Cambridge: Cambridge University Press, 1943 (and reprinted).

—— *What Happens in Hamlet.* Cambridge: Cambridge University Press, 1935 (and reprinted). A thorough piece on the tragedy, which is always interesting if, at times, debatable.

—— *The Essential Shakespeare.* Cambridge: Cambridge University Press, 1935 (and reprinted). A brief life of Shakespeare, with emphasis on what Shakespeare must have been like as a person, rather than on what he did.

Wright, Louis. *Shakespeare for Everyman.* New York: Washington Square Press, Inc., 1964.

Index

179